WHY?

FOREWORD BY DAVID JEREMIAH

WHY?

Answers to Weather
the Storms of Life

VERNON BREWER

BOOKS

PUBLISHED BY WORLD HELP, INC. FOREST, VIRGINIA

ISBN 0-9788041-1-2

World Help
1148 Corporate Park Drive
Forest, VA 24551
worldhelp.net

World Help exists to fulfill the Great Commission and the Great Commandment through partnering, training, helping and serving, especially in the unreached areas of the world.

Dedicated to each and every person
who faces a seemingly insurmountable challenge.
God knows what you are going through. He loves you
and has a plan for you to not only survive
but to thrive!

CONTENTS

ACKNOWLEDGEMENTS

I am wonderfully blessed by family and friends and would like to thank each one who offered encouragement, prayer and unconditional love during this incredible journey.

To my wife, Patty, and to my children, Noel, Nikki, Jenny and Josh ... thank you for your love, patience and support. You gave me the desire and determination I needed to fight.

To four wonderful grandsons: Riley, Adam, Bentley and Colin. God has big plans for you!

To my parents, Fred and Vivian Brewer. You gave me a foundation of faith and hope to build my future upon. The lessons you taught me by your example were my strength.

To my prayer team ... the friends, students and faculty/staff at Liberty University who lifted me and my family up in prayer throughout my illness. I am eternally grateful. A special thanks to Gary and Jan Aldridge, Dave and Jean Beck, Bill and Mary Bell, Mark DeMoss, Dwayne Carson, Eleanor Henderson Doody, Dave Earley, Dane Emerick, Jonathan Falwell, Pierre and Louanne Guillermin, Gary Habermas, Joe Hale, Mark Hine, David and Nancy Horton, Morgan Hout, Denny and Jane McHaney, Doug Oldham, Dave Randlett, Kathy Rusk, Mike Stewart, Tom Thompson, Elmer Towns, Bruce and Becky Traeger, Duane Ward,

Sumner Wemp, Harold Wilmington and Andy Zivonivich. You will never know the difference you made.

To Jerry Falwell, Ed Dobson and Ed Hindson. Thank you for anointing me with oil and praying; and thank you for your constant encouragement.

To four incredible doctors – John Halpin, Richard Lane, Gregg Albers and Stuart Harris. Thank you for taking care of the life that God placed in your hands.

To the entire World Help team, for sharing the passion and vision of World Help—the triumph of my trial. To my Executive Assistant, Nikki Hart … thank you for keeping me on track and organized.

To my editing team, Nancy Horton, Noel Yeatts, Eric Vess, Dawn Wilson, Kim Stewart and Shelly Roark for making it possible to share my journey and offer encouragement to those who are hurting through the written word.

And to God—my Comforter, Healer and Savior. Thank You for giving me strength, hope and an existence of divine purpose … more wonderful and fulfilling than I could ever imagine. It is my privilege and honor to share Your hope and help with those in need around the world.

FOREWORD

It seems to surprise some Christians that books like this one need to be written at all. So many these days seem to operate from the presupposition that Christians should not grieve, that Christians should not feel pain, that Christians should never suffer great trials or become deeply discouraged. Not only are such presuppositions unrealistic, they are unbiblical.

Many of the Psalms (and much of the rest of Scripture) are devoted to describing and encouraging believers whose backs are against the wall—believers enduring some kind of pain. The Bible is realistic about life. Suffering is inevitable.

Vernon Brewer understands why God allows suffering in a believer's life. He did not learn about it in a seminary classroom or by reading a book. He learned suffering in the hospital room and his teacher was cancer. I was there one day when he woke up from an important surgery. I saw the concern on the face of his parents and I heard the fear in Vernon's voice. But I also felt the quiet confidence that accompanied his faith in God.

Vernon and I have been friends for over 30 years. I have watched God shape his life and give him great influence in the kingdom. I have served on his Board of Directors and seen firsthand the impact he is making all around the world through World Help.

I think I know why God's favor is on his life. He has gone the way of Job. He has been tested in the furnace of suffering and made ready for his mission. Before God greatly uses any man, He crushes him. I used to pray that I could be the exception, but I have discovered that there are no exceptions.

Here's the good news! Vernon has chosen to write about the lessons he has learned and he has done it by bringing together his life experiences, his knowledge of God's Word and his personal journal entries.

When God allows suffering to enter our lives, it is important that we use that suffering to help others. II Corinthians 1:4 says, *"We encourage others with the encouragement wherewith we ourselves have been encouraged."*

When you have finished reading this book, you will be thankful that Vernon Brewer chose not to waste his suffering but to invest it in others for the glory of God.

Dr. David Jeremiah
Sr. Pastor,
Shadow Mountain Community Church
San Diego, California

INTRODUCTION

On August 29, 2005, Hurricane Katrina slammed into the Gulf Coast of the United States with such ferocity that President George W. Bush called it "one of the worst national disasters in our nation's history."[1] Millions of people were left homeless, stranded ... with only the clothes on their backs and no food or clean water. Thousands mourned the deaths of loved ones, while thousands more searched frantically for missing family and friends. They were completely and utterly without hope. As I walked through the streets and neighborhoods in the aftermath of this storm ... everyone I talked to asked the same question ... "Why? Why me? Why did the levies break? Why is help not coming sooner? Why ... why ... why?"

LIFE IS TOUGH ... IT'S A REAL STRUGGLE! Let's face it—the reality of life is that you are either entering a storm, going through a storm, or coming out of a storm. Some storms are worse than others ... but they are all inevitable.

My storm was cancer. What's yours?

Maybe you just received some bad news from the doctor and your hands still shake when you think about it. Or, your spouse left you, breaking your heart into so many pieces that you fear it will never be whole again. Possibly, you just lost your job and you don't know how you will make next month's rent. Or, maybe you found drug paraphernalia in your child's room. It could be that the love

"God whispers to us in our pleasure, speaks in our conscience, but shouts in our pain; it is His megaphone to rouse a deaf world."

—C.S. Lewis[2]

of your life just died. If so, I am truly sorry. Whatever your struggle, you probably feel hopeless and alone. And you probably have one question in your mind—"Why?"

On the other hand, you might be thinking, "Wait a minute, my life is going pretty well. I'm happy ... no big struggles or challenges."

I don't know your situation. But I do know this— sooner or later, **we all face storms. No one is exempt from problems.** I know ... I've been there.

My life was picture perfect—with a wife and family that I loved, a job I enjoyed and a ministry that was fulfilling— I had it all! Then the bottom dropped out. I was diagnosed with Hodgkin's Disease ... cancer! To be honest, I went through hell and, in doing so, felt the gamut of emotions— fear, rage, anxiety, resentment and more. It seemed that I fought God every step of the way. It was a time when all the trappings of life were stripped away and I came face-to-face with God.

I began to understand the reality of my physical limits and the hope of my spiritual destiny. When I was at my lowest, God was there for me ... even when I treated Him the worst. And He's there for you too.

My struggle with cancer was extremely difficult, but I can truly say that the most painful period of my life is now the most meaningful to me. I learned some specific principles of God's Word that comforted me, empowered me and opened my heart to a better life than I ever dreamed possible.

There are answers to the question, "Why?" But it can be a long and incredibly difficult learning experience.

You may not believe it now, but your storm could be viewed as a gift. Because of my struggles with pain and illness, I feel greater compassion, live more purposefully and enjoy the most amazing calling on my life—to give help and hope to those in great need.

Now, every day I try to live my life in such a way that I accomplish at least one thing that will outlive me and last for eternity. What a motivation!

Let's begin our journey from pain to healing ... from questions to answers ... from restoration to divine purpose ... and hopefully, you too can find the answers to "Why?"

When Hurricane Katrina swept through the Gulf Coast, the victims wondered if they would survive the ravages of the storm. Men, women and children who huddled in the darkness of New Orleans' Superdome felt abandoned and hopeless. But the storm passed. Many of those same individuals who suffered so greatly in the midst of the storm have found new beginnings and hope through the compassion of others ... through the spirit of determination ... and through the grace of God. Now, just over a year later as I sat watching the first NFL football game in the refurbished Superdome being televised, I thought about the hope that comes after the storm. Louisiana's team, The Saints, won the game decisively and this massive facility that had housed so much pain in the days following Katrina was now a place of victory and celebration. It was a symbol to me of the life and hope that can come after the storm.

1

WHEN THE
BOTTOM FALLS OUT

The Reality of Trials

"Consider it a sheer gift, friends, when tests and challenges come at you from all sides. You know that under pressure, your faith-life is forced into the open and shows its true colors. So don't try to get out of anything prematurely. Let it do its work so you become mature and well-developed, not deficient in any way."

—James 1:2-4, The Message

W ednesday evening, May 1, 1985, was the most difficult night of my life. Hours ticked by slowly and painfully as I lay in a room at Lynchburg's Virginia Baptist Hospital. I had just endured a lengthy surgery— doctors discovered and removed a five-pound tumor that was attached to my heart and lungs.

Later, the medical staff told me that if they had waited one more week to operate, it would have been too late. I was 38 years old and my happy, busy life had suddenly come to a grinding halt.

Over and over again I replayed the scene in my mind when I heard those fateful words ... "You have cancer."

"You have cancer!"

It was the moment that the bottom fell out of my world.

Only two weeks before, everything in my life was relatively normal. I was at the top of my game!

Married to the love of my life, Patty, and father to three amazing daughters—13-year-old Noel, 11-year-old Nikki, and 6-year-old Jenny—all was well. God had blessed me with a great job that I absolutely loved as the Dean of Students at Liberty University and had called me to preach the Gospel.

In fact, I am the first graduate of Liberty University. In 1973, I graduated in the top 10 of my class—which sounds like a great accomplishment until you know there were only eight graduates in that class! No one's name began with an "A" ... mine began with a "B", so with a stroke of luck, mine was the first name called to receive a diploma from Liberty University. I am proud of the education I received at Liberty where I learned the importance of vision and how to dream big!

So, I was sailing along in life as an obedient servant of God. What could go wrong?

Then, I came down with bronchitis and fought an intense battle with an illness that left me extremely weak. I was sick for nearly two months but never thought there was a deeper, more tragic reason behind it all.

One afternoon, exhausted, I lay down to rest. Suddenly, I felt a sharp, excruciating pain in my chest. I could hardly breathe. I learned later that the pressure from the tumor caused one of my lungs to collapse. After a rush to the emergency room and a few tests, I learned the devastating news.

The doctors diagnosed a rapidly growing form of Hodgkin's disease—a rare, malignant cancer affecting lymphatic tissue in my body. I needed immediate emergency surgery!

In that initial surgery, the doctors decided to take out approximately one third of my left lung in order to remove the entire tumor. But that wasn't the full extent of the bad news I would hear that day. During the surgery, they inadvertently severed the nerve to my vocal cords and diaphragm.

When I woke up, I found that my ability to speak normally was gone. The severed nerve made the simple task of speaking extremely difficult. I was forced to talk in whispers. I sounded more like a young child than a grown man. The doctors tried to give me hope; they said my vocal cords might heal in time. All I knew was that I could not preach without a voice. As a public speaker, I relied heavily on my voice. The thought of communicating with such a handicap was depressing and humiliating.

In one day, the security and normalcy of my entire world had disintegrated. I had no idea that ahead of me was a battle that included 18 surgeries and one and a half years of chemotherapy. All I knew as I lay in that hospital bed on May 1 was that my life had been turned upside down and it wasn't going to be righted any time soon.

> **JOURNAL ENTRY:**
>
> God, I've encouraged and prayed with others in times of crisis and tried to give them hope by reading the Bible. But this is different ... it's me.
>
> It's one thing to put my arm around someone and pray with them; it's quite another matter to cope with this overwhelming crisis in my own life. It's so hard. I feel like I'm drowning. All I can do is reach for You.

In those early weeks of my ordeal, everything was a blur. After the initial surgery, which was bad enough, they decided they had to immediately operate again to remove my spleen and see if my cancer had spread. I remember waking up after that second surgery on the cancer ward of the hospital ... I was groggy ... my chest felt like it was about to explode. The pain medication was wearing off and I was not doing well.

As soon as I was able to focus, I realized someone was sitting at the end of my bed. It was my good friend and former pastor, David Jeremiah. He had flown coast to coast from San Diego to Lynchburg to speak at Liberty University. There he sat, waiting for over an hour for me to wake up so he could let me know he was there and to pray for me. I don't remember his words, but I do remember him holding my hand and placing his other hand on my shoulder and literally crying out to God. What a moment—one that I will never forget!

During the months that followed, I endured many additional surgeries and surgical procedures. There were numerous complications. I spent weeks at a time in the hospital, went through a year and a half of debilitating radiation and chemotherapy, waded through countless agonizing hours of physical therapy and came close to death many times. I was also served up a few healthy helpings of humility.

Weeks in a hospital can strip away all of your dignity, modesty and control. With all the wounds, stitches, bandages ... I was sore and immobile. I remember one particular nurse that was very young, always had a smile on her face, and always had a word of encouragement for me. Every four hours she'd say, "Roll over," and give me an injection of morphine in my hip. She had the unfortunate task of bathing me, shaving me ... I was left with very little dignity.

After three days of tending to me, she bent down and whispered in my ear, "Dean Brewer, I'm one of your students, and I'm praying for you to get well." All I could do was pull the sheet over my head—I was never able to look her in the eye again!

There were good days and bad days—days I wanted to fight the disease, and some days when, feeling weak, I wanted to give up completely. There were lonely, dark days and nearly every one of them was painful.

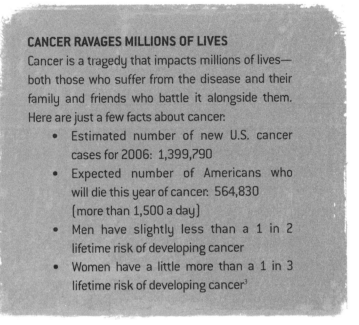

CANCER RAVAGES MILLIONS OF LIVES
Cancer is a tragedy that impacts millions of lives—both those who suffer from the disease and their family and friends who battle it alongside them. Here are just a few facts about cancer:

- Estimated number of new U.S. cancer cases for 2006: 1,399,790
- Expected number of Americans who will die this year of cancer: 564,830 (more than 1,500 a day)
- Men have slightly less than a 1 in 2 lifetime risk of developing cancer
- Women have a little more than a 1 in 3 lifetime risk of developing cancer[3]

And then, after months of excruciating pain and fear, the doctors finally gave me some good news. They told me I would survive.

A ray of hope! But just when I thought it was all over—as if facing cancer and chemotherapy were not enough—I developed more complications. The vein in my hand where I received powerful drugs collapsed and produced a chemical burn that destroyed the tissue and tendons of the entire upper part of my left hand. Doctors had to operate immediately ... again.

When I went into surgery, the plan was to do a simple skin graft—no big deal, or so I thought. When I woke up,

I discovered that the problem was much more serious than they expected. They had to attach my hand to skin and tissue from my side for a month in order for the blood vessels to reconnect. So picture this ... a grown man with the voice of a 6-year-old child, walking around with his hand attached to his side and stuck down the front of his pants. God has to have a sense of humor!

During my fight with cancer, I felt an almost overwhelming fear of the unknown and struggled to comprehend it all. My mind was consumed with questions: How could this have happened to me? What am I going to do? Will life pass me by? Can I survive?

But of all the thoughts and fears running through my head, one simple word stood above them all ... *WHY?*

∽

The fact is that no one is exempt from problems. I believe there are three types of people:

Those facing problems now.

Those who have just faced problems.

Those about to face problems.

The question is not "if" we will fall into a trial but rather "when."[4] Problems are only a phone call or an X-ray away. Difficulties in life are a given. They always have been.

In the 1st Century, members of the fledgling Christian Church experienced persecution that is almost mind-boggling. In his letters to them, James, one of the fathers of the early Church, didn't waste any time getting right to the

"You will be wounded. Just because this battle is spiritual doesn't mean it's not real; it is, and the wounds a man can take are in some ways more ugly than those that come in a firefight. To lose a leg is nothing compared to losing heart; to be crippled by shrapnel need not destroy your soul, but to be crippled by shame and guilt may."

—John Eldredge[5]

tough but very relevant issue for the times—trials. He was writing to a group of people who were well-acquainted with personal pain. Many of them had already faced severe trials, losing their homes, their jobs and their security. In fact, these believers had to literally flee Jerusalem for their own safety!

The truth is that as believers, the enemy of our soul is always challenging us and putting our faith to the test. Life's storms give us the opportunity to examine and prove our beliefs—both to ourselves and to the world.

Job is the biblical poster child for tragedy and triumph. He lost everything there was to lose, except for his life! All his livestock, property, his servants, his children and his health were destroyed.[6]

Was he being punished? No. God Himself declared Job as "blameless and upright."[7] So why was Job, God's faithful servant, taken from great wealth and success to the depths of torment? It was a series of tests instigated by Satan.

Satan wanted to prove to God that Job was a sinner who only believed God for what he could get out of it. God, on the other hand, had faith in the sincerity of Job's righteousness. He did not allow the dark storms to see Job fail … He allowed them to let Job shine!

And Job did not disappoint.[8] Through his stormy situation, Job's faith was strengthened, he learned about his own character and he grew closer to God. And in the end, God restored all that Job had lost and more.

Job had no idea why he was going through tragedy; he just trusted that God was in control. But there was a greater spiritual purpose behind his pain. Not all trials are like Job's … there are different kinds with different purposes and reasons.

In my burning desire to find out why life's storms come our way, I studied the different types of emotional and physical battles.

Guess what I learned? Sometimes, it's our own fault. Really! We reap what we sow, that's just the way life works.[9] God has promised to forgive our sins, but we still have to face the consequences of our actions.[10] Many of the stormy whirlwinds that come into our lives come as a result of our own disobedience, bad habits or actions.

But not every trial is a result of our own decisions. Spiritual trials come from simply living a godly life. If you are a true disciple of Christ, you will be out of step with society. Jesus was persecuted, so it shouldn't be surprising when we are too.[11]

The amazing truth of this statement became more vivid to me shortly after my hand surgery. I did not leave the house for an entire month, except to go to the doctor. I was afraid someone would see me. So, I found myself home alone on Easter Sunday, feeling sorry for myself.

In the midst of my wallowing, I suddenly realized, "Wait a minute—Jesus had a wound in His hand, and I

J-O-Y IN THE MIDST OF TRIAL?

James, a self-proclaimed servant of Christ, shared several practical principles with members of the early Church on how to benefit from trials. One that is as relevant and important for us today as it was for early believers is his advice to maintain joy in the midst of pain.[12]

Joy over tribulations? You gotta be kidding! I know how hard it is to remain positive when your life is in turmoil.

I remember like it was yesterday—the feeling I had each time we drove to my chemo session. I had to make myself go in ... and sometimes only found the strength after my wife Patty prayed with me at the door.

No, James is not saying that trials like this should be a joyful experience. Not at all. And that is definitely not the message I want to give you.

But James is saying that we should step back from our problems ... take a look at the big picture ... and rejoice at the beneficial results of our trial.

Your trial can become your friend when it drives you closer to God!

The joy James recommends is the ability to look beyond our circumstance and see the opportunity to become more like Christ.

It's true that you cannot know what will happen tomorrow, the next day or in the next year of your life. But one thing you can know right now, beyond a shadow of a doubt, is that God loves you and He has a divine plan for you. Hold onto that love, let it grow and take root in your heart. When you do, you will find the faith you need to look past your trial and grow closer to the Heavenly Father who loves you. You will be strengthened so you can "count it all joy."

have a wound in my hand. Jesus had a wound in His side, and I have a wound in my side."

What a clear picture! That Easter, home alone with my hand sewn to my side and two open wounds, I prayed, "God, thank You that this Easter, in a very small way, I can identify with the suffering that Jesus went through. Thank You for allowing me to identify with Christ."

✷

Just as in the early days of the Church, persecution for faith is still a daily reality for many believers around the world. Their trials are unimaginable.

In fact, according to Persecution.org, there are 200 million Christians suffering for their faith every day, from Cuba to North Africa to the Muslim Middle East, India and the rest of South Asia, North Korea, China, Vietnam and Indonesia. Many believers are arrested, beaten, starved and even murdered for their faith.[13]

An estimated 160,000 Christians are martyred each year worldwide![14]

In Poso, Indonesia, teenage girls suffered the ultimate persecution for confessing Christ. Three Christian high school students were on their way to school when they were viciously attacked and beheaded by radical Islamists. The head of one of the girls was deposited in front of the nearby Evangelical church. Two others were attacked as well but survived … despite the fact that their throats were slit. Soon after, two other young Christian girls were shot point blank in the head with pistols near a church.[15]

Not long ago, I was in Vietnam where I met a 35-year-old pastor. He had only been a Christian for a year but became a pastor because there was no one else to assume this responsibility. He had already experienced great persecution. He was beaten many times … as well as his wife. The authorities burned down his house because he would not forsake Christ. He built a tent and they burned that down also.

He is now living in another tent with his wife and four children. Recently his wife was once again severely beaten … this time she was pregnant and lost her baby. Most of us will never be called upon to face trials of this magnitude, but for many of our brothers and sisters, it is a common reality.

The story of another brave man who was severely tested for his faith made a deep impression on my life. His name is Cornel Iova.

I was preaching in Romania several years ago. Pastor Cornel asked me to go with him to a village church. He was so excited because it would be the first baptismal service in 50 years. On the way there, he told me how the Communist officials had torn the building down three times … and all three times the church members united and rebuilt it. We baptized many people and saw many come to Christ that day. It was a glorious day!

The pastor told me that day was historic for another reason. "It's the first anniversary of the death of my wife," he said. When I asked how, he told me she had died of cancer. He knew I was a cancer survivor and I asked him to tell me about it.

"She was diagnosed with acute leukemia. Some medical doctors from Great Britain felt they could spare her life with a bone marrow transplant surgery, but that delicate surgery could not be done in Romania. They offered to pay her expenses to come to London and perform the surgery free of charge!

"When she went to get her visa, the Communist officials told her they would let her go to England on one condition ... that she renounce her faith in Jesus Christ. She did not hesitate. She looked those officials in the eye and said, 'I *can not* do what you ask ... I *will not* do what you have asked.' And with her head held high, she turned and walked out. And in a few months ... she was gone." What bravery and dedication!

I am inspired and touched by Christians around the world who endure so much just to serve Jesus Christ. They face unbelievable struggles and challenges every single day.

So, we have "reap what we sow" trials and "spiritual" trials. But maybe the most difficult kind of trial to accept is the "senseless" trial. The problem is that there is simply no rational or logical reason for this kind of ordeal.

∾

This is the kind of trial Job faced! His friends were convinced that Job was facing a personal storm because of hidden sin in his life. His wife was certain it was God's fault.

WHEN ANSWERS AREN'T ENOUGH
By Scott Wesley Brown

You have faced the mountains of desperation
You have climbed, you have fought, you have won
But this valley that lies coldly before you
Casts a shadow you cannot overcome

And just when you thought you had it all together
You knew every verse to get you through
But this time the sorrow broke more than just
your heart
And reciting all those verses just won't do

Instead of asking why did it happen
Think of where it can lead you from here
And as your pain is slowly easing, you can find
a greater reason
To live your life triumphant through the tears

When answers aren't enough, there's still Jesus
He is more than just an answer to your prayer
And your heart will find a safe and peaceful refuge
When answers aren't enough, He is there

When answers aren't enough, He's still there[16]

Job asked many of the right questions but still did not know the "why?" When answers aren't enough, we must choose to rely on faith in our heavenly Father ... even when we are hurting so bad that we don't think He's around.

When C.S. Lewis was grieving the loss of his wife, he wrote, "Where is God? . . . When you are happy, so happy that you have no sense of needing Him, so happy that you are tempted to feel His claims upon you as an interruption, if you remember yourself and turn to Him with gratitude and praise, you will be—or so it feels—welcomed with open arms. But go to Him when your need is desperate, when all other help is vain, and what do you find? A door slammed in your face, and a sound of bolting and double bolting on the inside. After that, silence. You may as well turn away. The longer you wait, the more emphatic the silence will become. There are no lights in the windows. It might be an empty house. Was it ever inhabited? It seemed so once. And that seeming was as strong as this. What can this mean? Why is He so present a commander in our time of prosperity and so very absent a help in time of trouble?"[17]

The truth is that God *is* with us ... always. And He cares.

A great spiritual leader once said, "God is too good to be unkind and He is too wise to be mistaken. And when we cannot trace His hand, we must trust His heart."[18]

It was a hard lesson, but I learned that no matter what type of trial I face, I must turn to God and trust Him for strength, wisdom and joy in the midst of it all. As songwriter Scott Wesley Brown wrote, "When answers aren't enough, there's still Jesus." **He can be trusted with our future**. He wants the best for us and has great plans and purpose for our lives.[19]

⌒

My life is a testament to this! After numerous skin grafts and liposuction on my hand to make it look as normal as possible, the raised scar still serves as a daily reminder of the gift of life and how God brought me through the ordeal of cancer.

Finally, through the miracle of modern medicine, doctors injected liquid Teflon into my vocal cords, enabling me to speak. Once again, there were complications. The first surgery was not successful, requiring a second operation.

My voice is still not completely normal ... but I can speak! People tell me I speak with a "tear"—that I sound like I'm choking up, ready to cry. I'm told my new voice makes me sound more sincere. To be honest, I don't think about it much anymore, and when I do, I am grateful to be able to speak at all and do what God called me to do.

When I faced cancer, I thought my life was over. I feared I would never speak again and that my ministry was over too. I did not know then what I know now—the greatest accomplishments of my life came *after* cancer, not before. God is so good!

When a trial comes your way, I cannot tell you that you will have all your questions answered. What I can tell you is that you will have good days, bad days, painful days, strong days, weak days and encouraging days. But you will never have days alone.

I realize that it is not always God's will to heal and that, in fact, eventually every one of us will die. I've attended the funerals of many of my friends that I have now outlived. Every time, I ask the same question … "Why?" Why God chooses to heal some and not others is a mystery. We don't know why. Sometimes there is no immediate or obvious answer to the question, "Why?" When those times come, we can know this: God is sovereign, God is loving, God is kind. And He knows "why."

God is there and His Word is true. He is working for your good. Paul, one of Christ's early followers, said it this way, "All things work together for good to those who love God."[20]

And no matter what type of trial **you** face, God is in control.

LIFE LESSONS LEARNED

The Reality of Trials

Do not be surprised or caught off guard by trouble in your life. It is a part of the human condition and can certainly be overcome by faith and trust in God.

Recognize that God is ultimately in control and that He

has your best interest at heart. We may not be able to see the reason for our trials and challenges. And we might not know the purpose right away, but rest assured that God is sovereign and is working behind the scenes for your benefit.

Avoid resentment, bitterness and envy. Determine to pass the test of life and spirit that you are embroiled in. Through the fire of adversity, you can grow and be transformed into the successful complete servant of God you were created to be!

2

MY
WEAKEST MOMENT

The Battle of Emotion

"So do not fear, for I am with you; do not be dismayed,

for I am your God. I will strengthen you and help you;

I will uphold you with my righteous right hand."

—Isaiah 41:10

I t was 6:00 p.m. on a Sunday evening. My family had, once again, gone to church without me. I was not healthy enough to go with them but sat at home alone, discouraged and depressed.

I was listening to the radio broadcast of our church's Sunday evening service when I became frustrated and angry. I reached over, turned off the radio, and walked to the kitchen to find something to soothe the pain in my throat—pain from radiation burns. All I found was milk, and that made me even angrier.

I slammed the refrigerator door, looked at the ceiling, and shaking my fist as if I was shaking it in the face of God, I blurted out, "God, I can't stand this another minute!"

Immediately, I realized what I had done. I had lashed out at God. I felt so guilty and embarrassed; it truly was my weakest moment.

I slowly shuffled my way to my office and sat down in

my chair. I just stared at the wall. I had never felt more alone in my entire life.

Finally my eyes caught the title of a book on the shelf—*Depression*. A pastor in Oregon who had suffered a nervous breakdown wrote it. He told how he dealt with the depression that accompanied the breakdown. Everything within me screamed, "You need to read this book now!"

I had never read it. Why read a book on depression if you aren't depressed? It seemed to me that that type of book would tend to depress a "normal" person. But I really felt like I needed to read it right then.

I realize that depression is a serious disease in itself and many times there are physical causes, so I'm certainly not suggesting that all a person needs to do in the face of depression is read a book. But God wanted me to read that book that night.

I read the entire book in one sitting and was encouraged by the author's transparent odyssey through the depths of depression. I gained strength from the many verses of Scripture he used in telling his story. In fact, I took out an

JOURNAL ENTRY:

On some days, like today, I can't even pray or read the Bible. I don't feel human, much less spiritual.

index card and wrote down the references.

On the other side of the card, I wrote down the steps the author took that delivered him from depression. When I finished reading and making my notes, I was so convicted that I slipped to my knees and humbly asked God to forgive me for my angry outburst. I prayed for forgiveness for my "pity party" and asked for God's much-needed help.

I stayed up even later that evening, thinking about what I had read. When I finally fell asleep, there was peace.

The next day I felt a little better. My wife urged me to get out of the house for a few hours. She suggested I go to the office, check my mail, and then come home if I did not feel well. Like a good husband, I did.

I was not in my office for five minutes when my assistant, Becky Traeger, called me. "There is a pastor on the line who would like to speak with you," she said. "He said it is personal and urgent, but he won't give his name. Do you want to take the call, or would you like for me to take a message?" Reluctantly, I said I would take the call.

I'll never forget his opening words. "I am suffering from acute depression," the pastor said. "Can you help me? I would rather not give my name, if that's all right."

He told me his story, and I listened. Then I remembered the index card in my shirt pocket. I pulled it out and shared verses from the Bible. It was exactly what he needed to hear. I turned the card over and shared principles and steps that he needed to take to get out of depression. About 30 minutes into the conversation, he asked me, "How do you know so much about this?"

I wanted to tell him that I had a Ph.D. in clinical psychology, but that wouldn't have been the truth and it was a serious conversation. Instead, I said, "Let me tell you what happened to me last night."

I told him about my weakest moment. When I finished, we were both weeping. He promised that he would seek professional help, then we prayed and said good-bye. To this day, I don't know his name.

When I arrived back home, I told my wife what happened, and she said, "See, there are *other* ways to preach, and God can still use you!"

But that's not the end of the story.

Later that day, I received a phone call from Morgan Hout, my dear friend who was then the Head Coach of Liberty University's football team. He said, "Vernon, we are having a party on campus tonight, and we would really like for you to attend. One of our graduates is playing in his first NFL game on Monday Night Football. We are going to watch it on the big screen."

I said, "Coach, I am not up for a party." He asked me to at least come for a few minutes because it would really mean so much to the players. Reluctantly, I agreed to come.

When I arrived, I headed to the food and beverage area to get something to drink. A huge lineman—I don't even know his name—walked up to me and said, "Can I speak with you?"

We sat down and he said, "I want you to know that I pray for you every day. After every practice, Coach has the entire team take a knee on the 50-yard line and pray that God will heal you. I want you to know that I believe God will heal you, but I need to ask you something. Last night," he said, "I was driving back on campus and I got this strong urge to pray for you. I have never experienced anything like that before—it wouldn't go away. I didn't know what to do, so I pulled my car off the road and began praying for you for the longest time. When I finished, I noticed that it was a little after 6:00 p.m."

He paused, and then said, "Do you mind me asking if anything unusual was going on last night at 6:00?"

It suddenly dawned on me ... I was able to connect all the dots.

In my weakest moment, when I was angry at God and felt alone, depressed, forgotten—when I could not even pray for myself, God was there. He did not forget me. He loved and cared about me so much that He had a football player pray for me when I could not pray for myself.

When I hit rock bottom, I had never been lower, I had never been lonelier and I had never been more depressed in my whole life. But at the time of my greatest need, God was there just as He promised.[21]

At the time of my greatest depression, He was there to comfort, give grace and strengthen my weakness. He'll be there for you too.

When you come to that place of being all alone, when you've exhausted all your human resources—that is when you will find a greater strength than you ever believed possible. That is where you will win the battle of emotion … one of the most vicious battles of your life.

❧

I'll never forget the first time I watched the fight between Rocky Balboa and Apollo Creed in the movie, *Rocky*. I winced and grimaced with every punch he took. Rocky's opponent pummeled the inexperienced boxer over and over again with punishing blows. It didn't take long before the young fighter's face was broken, bloody and swollen. His ribs, stomach … every part of his body was taking a beating.

Apollo, the reigning heavyweight boxing champion, knocked Rocky to the floor of the ring over and over again. But each time, the battered but determined boxer found the strength to get up. It was too brutal. He could not survive another blow. Why did he keep getting up? How could he keep getting up? Soon, I was yelling at the screen right along with his trainer Mickey, "Just stay down Rocky, stay down!"

Finally, Apollo leveled one more crushing blow at Rocky. He went down for the count one last time—one, two, three, four…

When we endure a trial, we feel about like Rocky looked as he lay on the floor of that boxing ring. I know I do. Even without the physical scars to show it, challenges and struggles can leave us battered and broken—just like with Rocky's boxing epic.

LIFE APPLICATION — SURVIVING THE BOMB

So, how can you cope with the "bombshell experience" or help someone you love through it?

Take time to think through the situation. Pray and take the time to sort through the aftermath of that initial bomb dropping into your life. Worrying can cause more harm than good.

Realize that God is not punishing you. God loves you so much that He wants to see you conformed in the image of Christ. Try to understand that He is doing a deep work in your life and that His plan and purpose may be beyond what you can comprehend at this moment.

Just be there. The best way you can help someone you love who is going through the initial heartache and heartbreak of that bombshell experience is to let them know you are there and want to help. I remember so vividly, friends who didn't say much ... they were just there. They let me know by their love and their presence that they cared. And that is so important.

More often than not, the most serious wounds we endure in life are those found on the inside ... the ones we suffer during a battle of emotion. And the despair we feel on the inside can be just as painful as a bloody, gaping wound to our bodies. An emotional beating can leave us weak, vulnerable, close to defeat like Rocky. But, unlike in a fictional story, our struggles are very real ... and the ending is being scripted by our actions and faith.

I went through several stages in this battle of emotion during my own personal struggle. More times than I can count, I wanted to tunnel under or go around to avoid the emotions that I needed to face. But now I know that it was a journey that I had to go through in order to receive all the benefits. I fully believe that:

God will not change our circumstances until the circumstances that He's allowed in our lives change us.

The battle of emotions is nothing more than the process of transformation that starts in the mind.

STAGE 1: THE BOMBSHELL EXPERIENCE

This step begins the moment your world caves in around you. I remember vividly when the bombshell hit me. I was in the intensive care unit recovery room after my initial surgery. I was just coming to and they took the breathing apparatus out of my mouth. My wife, my good friend Gary Habermas and my pastor Jerry Falwell were standing by my bedside. I reached out and grasped Jerry's hand, asking him, "Is it cancer?"

"Yes," he replied. "But they think they got it all."

Jerry encouraged me and prayed with me, but the words continued to explode inside my head ... "Yes, you have cancer." I felt paralyzed from the force of those devastating words.

There are times in our lives when we receive a blow that seems impossible to bear. Such news can numb you, making it difficult to cope with reality or grasp the seriousness of the situation. It renders us helpless to make good decisions.

It can even be difficult to carry on conversations because of the overwhelming burden of worry and anxiety. I remember that in those first few days and weeks after receiving such devastating news, I felt very detached from reality.

STAGE 2: AN ILLUSION OF NORMALCY

Not long after the initial cave-in is step two ... pretending the nightmare never happened—or acting as if it will go away if you ignore it. Our human spirit, even after it has been racked with grief, has the remarkable ability to reestablish itself. But I learned from experience that nothing can be further from the truth than trying to pretend nothing is happening to you.

For several weeks, I tried to regain control of my life. I tried so hard to make decisions for myself, hoping that if I could just gain control, all of the pain would go away. Trust me ... it doesn't.

We cannot run from reality ... we cannot wish our circumstances away.

As I was trying to sweep my problems under the carpet and pretend that they didn't exist, God was gently whispering to me: "You can't run, Vernon. There is no need to run. I'm here and I'll help you."

I had to go through the painful realities of this emotional stage to recognize that holding back the tears, trying to fool myself and pretending the pain is not there is no solution at all.

STAGE 3: HITTING ROCK BOTTOM

When anger has played itself out and the storm has subsided, there is a new emotion that makes itself known in the lives of the troubled. It's an emotion that can be soft, sad and tender in its own way. But at the same time, like a monster ... it can be terrifying! The best way to describe this monster of emotion in my own life is *loneliness*. But even then, God was with me.

Sometimes rock bottom comes in the form of worry and anxiety.

One day I was alone in my hospital room—depressed, worried, wondering if I would survive ... wondering how my family would make it financially without me. I was alone and worried. At that moment, Jerry Falwell walked into my room and said, "Vernon, I can only stay a minute ... I'm in a board meeting across the street and we took a break. God wanted me to come over and tell you something. I don't want you to worry about your job—it will be there for you when you get well no matter how long it takes. I don't want you to worry about your salary—you'll continue to receive it while you're getting well. I don't want you to worry about your family—God forbid if anything should happen to you—I'll take care of them. I don't want you to worry about anything but getting well."

Jerry Falwell was a messenger from God. Few people ever get to see the side of Jerry I saw that day. I will always have a special love in my heart for Jerry—for what he did for me!

Whenever we hit rock bottom, God will be there to pick us up.

STAGE 4: A RUDE AWAKENING

In this stage of coping emotionally, reality sets in. You are hit with the full realization of what is happening to your life. Maybe you understand for the first time that your life will never be the same.

Five years after terrorists crashed two airplanes into the Twin Towers of the World Trade Center on September 11, 2001, killing 2,992 and shaking up the entire nation, victims and families are still learning to deal with the rude awakening of the impact this tragedy had on their lives.

I read recent news stories of how survivors are coping with the changes. One victim, Lynn Simpson, worked on the 89th floor of Tower One and made it out. Today, she still struggles.

She moved out of the city and into the Pennsylvania countryside and hasn't been on an airplane since 9/11. Lynn said she hates loud noises and has been diagnosed with post-traumatic stress.

ARE YOU LONELY?

There are so many lonely people, so many lonely Christians. Maybe you can say today, "I'm lonely and I'm not even facing crisis."

I believe with all my heart that God allows periods of loneliness in our lives to remind us that He can be our closest friend. I remember someone saying that loneliness becomes your friend when it forces you to enjoy your fellowship with God as much as you enjoy the fellowship of others.

I enjoy the fast-paced, hectic activity of life. I enjoy the fellowship of friends. I just enjoy people! So, it's very difficult for me to slow down and be still. It's hard to slow down and just enjoy fellowship with God.

But I'm learning that loneliness is not my enemy, but my friend. The truth is that we are never really alone. We are never at a place that God is not if we have a relationship with Jesus Christ.

"I guess I was confident that I could get my life back," she said. "And as time went on, I realized I was not going to be able to get my life back. I had been changed. I'm trying to find myself again. And trying to find a new person, because I will never be the old person. And that makes me sad, but I'll be a new person."[22]

Victims like Lynn were forever changed by the events of 9/11 ... in fact, our entire nation was impacted by that horrible tragedy. Tragedy and circumstances change people and transform lives. It's a fact of life.

The good news is that God can create something new and wonderful from the broken pieces of our lives.[23]

STAGE 5: ACCEPTANCE

This is the most important stage of all ... acceptance. We must accept that what is happening is from God. Now, that's not fatalism. That's not giving up. It's not saying, "Whatever will be ... will be." On the contrary, it's a very active faith in God.

Through acceptance, we believe God's Lordship over our lives and allow Jesus Christ to have control and work in our lives.

I learned that acceptance is so necessary. When I began cooperating with God and trusting what He was doing in my life, I found peace. I had come to a place where I said, "I'm not going to quit. I'm not going to give up."

There is hope. As long as there's a God in heaven ... as long as Jesus is Lord and sits on the throne in heaven, there is hope.

We can battle discouragement and loneliness and win. We don't have to allow our emotions to control us. We can control our emotions. We can make it through our weakest moments with God's help.

"We shouldn't deny the pain of what happens in our lives.

We should just refuse to focus only on the valleys."

—*Charles Swindoll*[24]

In fact, it is in our times of weakness that we can truly shine.

I remember one day when I was particularly ill and just didn't want to go to work. I especially didn't want to go to chapel that day. The doctor had told me that because of my chemotherapy, my chances of catching a cold or the flu were greater and that I should avoid being around a lot of people. And to be honest, just walking across campus was an ordeal that left me drained. But, at the last minute, I decided to go.

I entered the building quietly and went up onto the platform where I normally sat. It took a lot of effort, but I made it. The service was fairly uneventful ... until the very end.

After chapel was over, a student walked up to me. What he told me made my every effort to get there that day worthwhile.

"I've got my car packed," he said. "I'm discouraged and homesick. I've got financial problems and I was on my way to the business office to quit school. I just wanted to come to chapel to say good-bye to my friends."

Then, with tears in his eyes, he continued. "But seeing you here … If you can face your crisis and not quit, then I can face what I'm going through without quitting. I'm staying in school! Thank you."

We should not count ourselves out just because we are struggling with depression, anxiety, disappointment or fear. Hang in there!

Sooner or later, we all find ourselves face down in the ring, waiting for the count, just like Rocky. On some days, we feel like we are beaten down by life and on the losing end in the battle of emotions. That is when we must get back up! Rocky got up after that last blow knocked him to the ground. He was battered, bruised and beaten, but he went the distance. We all can.

When people ask me how I coped with cancer, I tell them, "One day at a time." I got up every day. I trusted God for that day … that moment. I didn't rely on my own strength—I had none. I plugged into the Word, leaned on my friends and family, prayed and rested in God's arms. And I found out that the weakest moments of my life can also be the times when I find my greatest strength in God.[25]

LIFE LESSONS LEARNED

The Battle of Emotion

Don't be afraid to express your feelings and allow yourself to go through the range of emotions. Each step in your battle of emotions is part of the healing process.

Cope one day at a time. Don't try to take on your entire life ... live one day at a time. Minimize the bad days. Maximize the good days. Thank God for today and accept it.

Turn to God for strength. You don't have to be superhuman. We all face disappointment, depression and anxiety. But the key to overcoming is trusting in God.

3

AFRAID OF DYING

The Reason for Trials

"For God has said, 'I will never fail you. I will never forsake you.' That is why we can say with confidence, 'The Lord is my helper, so I will not be afraid.'"

—Hebrews 13:5-6, NLT

"Up until this point I have been doing well," I said. "Spiritually and emotionally, I have been strong. But I'm beginning to have fears and I cannot control my emotions—I'm crying all the time.

"I'm afraid of dying," I said. "Is that a satanic attack?"

Ed Dobson, my close friend and counselor, looked at me and said, "No, Vernon, you have a life-threatening and potentially terminal disease. That is reality!"

I was in the middle of one of the harder times during my battle with cancer. I experienced a great fear of dying— not so much because I wasn't prepared to die, but because I just loved life so much. I wanted to cling to it— I wasn't ready to let go. To be honest, I was terrified of letting go.

The fear was debilitating, crippling. Essayist H.P. Lovecraft said, "The oldest and strongest emotion of mankind is fear, and the oldest and strongest kind of fear is fear of the unknown."[26]

If you face the unknown today in your family, your career, your future because of a seemingly insurmountable challenge, the advice my friend gave to me that day can apply to your life too.

"Vernon," Ed said, "you have one of three alternatives, as I see it. First, you can get angry with God, quit, turn your back on God, and turn your back on Christianity."

I knew immediately that wasn't an alternative I wanted to pursue.

"The second option is that you can run from reality," he said.

"You can run from the reality that it is appointed unto man once to die.[27] You can hide from that responsibility and only fool yourself."

I knew that neither of those two alternatives were really what God wanted in my life. I was eager to hear Ed's third option.

"The third thing you can do is accept these circumstances from God," he said. "You know circumstances don't make us what we are. Each of us faces our own set of circumstances, our own set of difficulties in coping with life and living the Christian life. Those circumstances do not make us what we are; they merely reveal the true character of who we are."

In my heart, I knew what God was saying: "Accept what I am doing. Wait on me. Be patient. Let me work in your life."

I knew I had to come to the place where I was willing to die. I had to come to the place of acceptance of death as one of the alternatives.

It made sense ... it was the right thing to do. But knowing that didn't make acceptance any easier. I remember having fears, and I guess they were normal insecurities considering the circumstances. I wondered ... "What will happen to my wife? What will happen to my children? What will happen to my ministry?" The fear of knowing life would go on without me was painful and traumatic.

I remember walking down the hall at night and hearing my daughters cry themselves to sleep. It tore my heart out. I would close the door to my room and weep. Knowing my children were suffering was much worse than any physical pain I was in.

JOURNAL ENTRY:

Lord, You are in control of my life, You are Lord of my wife, my children, my career and my future. If You take me, You will take care of my wife. God, I believe that if You take me, You will take care of my children and my ministry. All these things that I worry about, God, I give them to You. And right now, I acknowledge that You are Lord.

"I'll never walk my daughters down the aisle at their weddings," I thought. "I'll never hold my grandchildren. I'm going to die. Why is this happening to me?"

But when I left Ed after our conversation about my fear of dying, I knew I could not be angry with God; I could not run from reality. I had to face what God was doing in my life and accept it as from the Lord. I had to come to the place where I was willing to let go of my life and be willing to face death—death to my own desires, wants and wishes.

I was willing to wait on the Lord to renew my strength and complete His purposes in my life.

As I drove home, I poured my heart out to God. I told Him that I trusted Him to handle my future and take care of my family. I trusted Him with my life … and my death. I turned my greatest fear over to Him. In that prayer, I literally died to myself and my selfishness. What freedom it brought!

That prayer became a reality in my life and with it I turned a corner in my spiritual health. It gave God greater freedom to nurture and strengthen me. It lifted a burden off my shoulders and I believe it will do the same for you.

I certainly don't know what tomorrow will bring. So, I thank God for today, and I thank Him for all of my yesterdays. I understand that I'm not promised I'll even have tomorrow, so all I can do is give Him complete control of today.

"Patience and perseverance have a magical effect before which difficulties disappear and obstacles vanish."

—*John Quincy Adams*[28]

༄

One of the big questions in my life as I fought cancer was: "Why does God allow storms or trials in our lives?" I've studied why Christians suffer, why bad things happen to good people. And I learned that there is a purpose.

Again, why does God allow trials in our lives? So that He can examine, scrutinize and put our faith to the test.[29] "Testing" means "proving" or "trying"—the same kind of testing as a refiner's fire that burns out all the alloys from precious metal. All the impurities must be burned away to get to "the good stuff." It's the same with you and me.[30]

God allows testing in our lives for good ... to prove the quality of our character. As we commit ourselves to Him, He allows our impure motives and conduct to be removed from our lifestyles.

According to James, the "testing" develops "perseverance."[31] Perseverance is the prize. It can also be described as "patience" and "endurance."

Perseverance, patience and endurance—three qualities that are necessary for victory in our lives—just don't grow

HELPING OTHERS PERSEVERE

If you know someone who is facing a trial ... don't ever underestimate the power of encouragement. We can help those we love and care about endure trials through our kindness, thoughtfulness and encouragement.

You may feel awkward and don't know what to say—there are times when very little should be said. But it's important to be there for your friend or loved one.

God has blessed me with a best friend in life ... Tom Thompson. Tom and I met while he was in college. He shared with me a spiritual struggle he was going through at the time. We prayed together and became instant friends. For 10 years, we traveled together in an itinerant ministry. We spoke in hundreds of churches and thousands of public schools. In 1984, our ministries took different paths. I went back to Liberty University as Dean of Students. Tom became the Executive Pastor with David Jeremiah at Shadow Mountain Community Church in San Diego, California. It was only nine months later when I was diagnosed with cancer.

Tom was always there. He called me regularly. He visited me often. He always had a word of encouragement. He sent me books and inspirational tapes. He would always call me with the latest joke he had heard in hopes of lifting my spirits. He sent me gift certificates to take my wife out to dinner. He wouldn't let up—he was there for me!

overnight; they must be developed.

There are two things we need to know about the characteristic of perseverance that God wants for our lives.

First, perseverance is not deliverance *FROM* trials ... it is endurance *IN* trials. We have a tendency to think that any time a problem comes our way, all we have to do is pray and God will instantly deliver us from all our problems.

Of course, sometimes God will do that to prove His power. There are plenty of examples of miracles in the Bible and modern day testimonies to prove that God has the power to take care of any need. But most of the time, God wants to produce patience in our lives. And patience is not being delivered *from* the problem. Patience is learning to *endure* the problem.

Patience is not deliverance, it's endurance! We must persist and be dogged in our determination to find God's will and purpose in the trial. Success comes to the persistent in any arena.

Walt Disney was turned down 302 times before he got financing for his dream of creating the "Happiest Place on Earth." Colonel Sanders spent two years driving across the United States looking for restaurants to buy his chicken recipe. He was turned down 1,009 times![32] They stuck with it and survived the disappointments.

Secondly, we need to realize that endurance is a process. The acquisition of endurance is not something that happens immediately once and for all.

Wouldn't it be great if we only faced one test in life ...

"Success is not final, failure is not fatal; it is the courage to continue that counts."

—Winston Churchill[33]

only one test in high school ... only one test in college? Unfortunately, that's not how it works.

Human nature tries to bypass painful circumstances. But circumstances don't make us *what* we are. They reveal *who* we are. We may not be able to change the circumstances in our lives. We can, however, choose how we respond to them.

One day, not long after surgery, I received a long distance phone call from my father. He said, "Son, I have a verse to encourage you today."

"What is it?" I asked. "I could use a little encouragement."

"Isaiah 40:31," he replied. *'But those who wait on the LORD will find new strength. They will fly high on wings like eagles. They will run and not grow weary. They will walk and not faint.'*

My first response was, "Dad, I know that verse. I've heard that verse. I've quoted that verse. I've even preached from that verse. That's what I'm asking God to do ... to help me fly high on wings as an eagle."

"Wait a minute, son," he replied. "What does that verse

say you must do *before* you can fly high as an eagle?"

"Well, it says you need to renew your strength."

"And what do you need right now in your life more than anything else?" he asked.

"Strength."

"So, where will you get that strength? How will you get that strength? And how does God want you to receive that strength?" he asked.

"By *waiting* on the Lord," I said. Do parents always have to be right?

It's very difficult to wait on the Lord. I was very good at serving the Lord. I was great at church attendance and worship ... but not so good at waiting.

Learning to wait on God and spend time in His presence takes work.

The benefit is that in the face of fear, uncertainty and anxiety, we can be strengthened as we wait on the Lord!

Whether we are afraid of dying ... losing our children ... or being all alone, we can hand our fear and our situation over to God. We don't have to waste valuable time worrying about the unknown. World War II concentration camp survivor Corrie Ten Boom said, "Worry does not empty tomorrow of its sorrow; it empties today of its strength."[34]

We can rest in the assurance that there is a purpose for our trials and wait on Him to bring it to pass.

God has a purpose and a plan for your trials and has promised to never leave you as you face the greatest battles of your life. You don't need to fear death, loneliness, bankruptcy or anything else. Why? Because God will be right there with strength and guidance.[35]

LIFE LESSONS LEARNED

The Reason for Trials

Know that there is a purpose for your trial and a plan for your life. God wants to develop in you the patience, perseverance and endurance you need for victory.

You must go through the process to receive the benefits. There are no shortcuts through tough circumstances. It is in your circumstances that you will find out what you are made of!

When you wait on God, you will find strength. Spend time in prayer. Keep serving. Focus on your relationships with others and with God.

4

MIRACLE DAY
OF PRAYER

The Power of Prayer

"Are any among you sick? They should call for the elders of the church and have them pray over them, anointing them with oil in the name of the Lord."

—James 5:14, NLT

Early on in my battle with cancer, I took a turn for the worse. The radiation treatments no longer worked and my doctor switched me to a 12-month aggressive regimen of chemo. Debilitated, I neared death on several occasions.

At that time, I served as Dean of Students at Liberty University and led the student missions program. We took hundreds of students to the mission field every year. My struggle with the disease affected the entire campus, and the students became my support group. They encouraged me with their cards, phone calls and visits to my office, just to tell me they were praying for me. They kept me going.

Two of my good friends, Gary Aldridge and Dwayne Carson—who served as campus pastors—saw my deterioration and wanted to do something extreme. They organized a campus-wide "Miracle Day of Prayer" to ask God to heal me.

A few days before Thanksgiving, on November 25, they arranged a voluntary 24-hour prayer chain of students and staff. They asked everyone to sign up for one or more hours to pray and set up a candlelight prayer vigil in the small chapel on Liberty University's campus.

Day and night for 24 hours straight, nearly 3,000 students filled the chapel. Most of them had never done anything like that in their lives.

I don't know all their names, but I am so thankful for each one of those young men and women who prayed for my healing.

I attended as many of those one-hour prayer vigils as my stamina would allow—amazed to see those students' faith. They put their arms around me, laid their hands on me, and connected with me in ways that I've never forgotten. Fatigued, I went home around midnight.

I found out the next morning that the chapel was packed all night long. In fact, the largest attendance occurred between 2:00 a.m. and 6:00 a.m. When I meet people who tell me they remember the Miracle Day of Prayer and they prayed for me, they almost always tell me they prayed between those early morning hours.

God healed me from cancer. For that, I give Him all the glory and honor! The battle I endured tried my patience. Many depressing, lonely times surrounded me; it was the most difficult trial of my life. In reality, God's healing came through many means. He healed me through the words of friends, the prayers of strangers, the medical care of doctors and by His unseen hand directing my path. And I know

To this day, I still meet people all over the world who tell me,

"I remember, as a college student, the Miracle Day of Prayer

we had for you. I was one of those students in the prayer

chapel that prayed for your healing."

"Do you remember what time you prayed?" I ask. They

always remember.

without a doubt that prayer was an integral part of my healing.

I will never know for sure—at least not until I get to heaven—if that Day of Prayer was the specific day God used to heal me. For now, I believe it was. I believe God honored the faith of thousands of students and gave them a tangible answer to prayer they would never forget. I believe I am alive today, in part, because of the faith of those students and for their "powerful and effective prayers."

◦

Prayer is one of the unexpected blessings to come from facing life's challenges. Storms in life can bring us closer to God. When we are struggling, we have the opportunity for a renewed connection with God through prayer. As I engaged in the most devastating battle of my life, I came to

MY FRIEND'S PRAYER

One of my dearest friends in life is Elmer Towns. I met Elmer at a Sunday School conference in Kansas City, when I was a young college student. I wasn't really walking with God at that time. A few months later, while living in Hawaii, Elmer came to Honolulu for another conference and our paths crossed again. I taught him how to surf and snorkel. He taught me how to love God. We became good friends. Later, as a student at Liberty University, he became my teacher and mentor.

That night in the chapel, on our knees, Elmer prayed with me. He was intense. I had never heard him pray that urgently before. His prayer gave me hope. He put his arm around me and encouraged me. Every year since that night, Elmer has sent me a card of encouragement to mark that anniversary. I treasure those cards—I treasure my friendship with Elmer Towns. Occasionally, Elmer and I find time to play a round of golf together. Every time we do, we talk about that night, on our knees, in the prayer chapel—the 24-hour Miracle Day of Prayer.

realize the need for constant communion with God through prayer ... I found encouragement in quiet times spent with the Lord ... and I discovered the power of intercession.

I learned to run to God in times of trouble and to hold

on to the open lines of communication long after the desperation fades.

David Jeremiah takes the benefits of prayer a step further in his book, *Prayer, the Great Adventure*. He says believers are "missing out on something wonderful and indescribable" by not praying. He wrote: "I have found that prayer is the most wonderful gift in God's great bag of blessings. It is the great adventure of the Christian faith."[36]

Prayer should be a given in a believer's life. It is as essential to our spirit as the air we breathe is needed for our bodies to function. Prayer has a priceless role in our walk of faith and offers some incredible benefits to us as believers—communication with God, encouragement and power.

∽

Dave Earley is my good friend. We worked together at Liberty University during my battle with cancer. Dave was part of my support group ... he was there for me. Some days, he even drove me to the hospital for my chemo treatments. He always kept my spirits up. But on August 18, 1991, Dave was faced with his own trial and his story illustrates the incredible power of constant prayer in our lives.

Dave woke up that morning in August with what he thought was a serious case of the flu. He felt terrible with pain in his joints and muscles and a severe headache that just wouldn't go away. But more symptoms began to invade his body. He became allergic to many normal things, experienced difficulty communicating, and had trouble sleeping.

Also, every afternoon, about the same time, his throat would become so sore he could hardly swallow. He lost over 18 pounds in just three weeks.

But the most debilitating symptom was fatigue. He was exhausted 24 hours a day. It took all his strength just to make himself turn over in bed. Once, he couldn't muster enough strength to walk to the bathroom, so he crawled.

He couldn't play with his three children (all boys under the age of 5) and was forced to neglect his wife because it took all of his abilities to just take care of himself.

Dave suffered from guilt and pain for 10 months before he sought help. He was diagnosed with Chronic Fatigue Immune Deficiency Syndrome.

"I was frustrated from being the slave of my pain and fatigue. I was frustrated because I was a goal-oriented person who was now unable to pursue any goal other than survival. I was frustrated because when I was home, I did not have the strength to get off the couch to play with my boys. I was frustrated because my fatigue was wearing my wife out.

"But more than anything, I was frustrated with God. The only response I could get from Him was silence. . . blank, empty, hollow, deafening silence. Day after day I asked for deliverance, for at least an explanation or at the very least, a time frame for my agony. (I looked in the Book of Job for a time frame. How long did he suffer? I even asked some of the best Bible scholars in the country that question and they all had the same answer, "The Bibles does not say.") Yet, day after day, week after week, month after month, God said nothing. My illness stretched into years, yet on this issue I received only silence.

"For a time I prayed on diligently, an hour a day for months. Yet God was still silent. It felt like He had abandoned me and I did not even know why. My soul was dry and my heart broken. I hate to admit it, but eventually I reasoned that if God would no longer speak to me then I would not speak to Him, and for a period of weeks, I had almost no prayer life."

Being a Christian, Dave knew this was wrong. As children of God, we must talk to our heavenly Father. Little by little he began by praying prayers of thanksgiving. Then, singing prayers of praise. He began to feel better.

Because he had been a child of God for a long time, he decided he couldn't give up on Him now. So he began to tell God that even if he never got better, even if God never answered his prayers and never offered any explanation— he would always love Him. After this ... miraculously Dave began to get better.

"Getting better has been a very slow process. It has been almost 12 years since I first got sick and I still battle CFIDS every day. But, I am still getting better. I exercise almost an hour a day. I run three miles, three times a week. My wife and I frequently take up to a 30-mile bike ride on my day off. And the pain is much better. But even if I was not getting better, even if I only got worse, God would still be worth my loyalty and love. I deserve eternal death and He has given me eternal life and abundant life. Even if He never said another thing to me, did another thing for me, gave

JOURNAL ENTRY:

I don't believe that God is obligated to heal me because I prayed, but I do believe that God is able to heal me because I prayed.

another thing to me, He would still deserve all of the love and devotion I can give Him.

"And one day I will be 'all better.' When I say, 'better' I mean, 'better!' I will walk the streets of Heaven in a brand new, pain-free, tireless, non-allergic, glorious, incorruptible body. No more fatigue! No more weakness! No more exhaustion! No more pain! I not only will be 'as good as I used to be,' but I will be much better than I ever imagined!"[37]

Dave discovered that prayer is our spiritual lifeline. Prayer gives us encouragement and hope.

∽

Whether we are struggling with challenges of life or not, it's so important to set aside time daily to spend communicating with God through prayer. He longs for a close, personal relationship with each and every one of us.

I can think of no greater comfort than prayer in my daily life—especially in times of need.

"Everything we do that's worth doing; everything God wants to do in the church; everything God wants to do in your life; He has subjugated it all to one thing: Prayer."

—David Jeremiah[38]

I have vivid memories of the day when I learned that they were going to have to operate on me for possible cancer. The doctor called me on the phone and said, "We've reviewed your CAT scan and your chest x-rays." By his tone, I knew immediately that I was facing a serious set of circumstances.

My first response was to ask Jerry Falwell if he would mind anointing me with oil and praying a prayer of faith for me. I'll never forget that meaningful time when—together on our knees with Ed Dobson and Ed Hindson—we cried out to God for His healing. It was the most intense prayer meeting I have ever experienced; it was a powerful, emotional experience.

When I have a time of difficulty, I go back to that night and remember that I trusted God. I asked God, by faith, for healing.

This moment of prayer and agreement has been one of the most encouraging images of my life. I revisit it often for strength … I rely on it … I rest in it. This prayer and thousands like it have sustained me and I challenge you to tap into the encouraging hope found through prayer.

Don't hesitate to find a prayer partner or prayer group in your time of need. Whether it's your pastor, fellow believers, church elders or a Bible study group, don't be afraid to ask for prayer. When you share your burdens and pray for each other in unity, not only will you be encouraged, but you will also see results![39]

In 1999, a controversial study was published in the Archives of Internal Medicine that gives just a hint of the power of prayer. Researchers studied the impact of intercessory prayer on cardiac patients at St. Luke's Hospital in Kansas City, Missouri.

"Prayer may be an effective adjunct to standard medical care," says cardiac researcher William Harris, Ph.D., who headed the study. His team examined the health outcomes of nearly 1,000 newly admitted heart patients at St. Luke's. The patients, who all had serious cardiac conditions, were randomly assigned to two groups. Half received daily prayer for four weeks from five volunteers who believed in God and the healing power of prayer. The other half received no prayer in conjunction with the study.

The volunteers were all Christians and the participants were not told they were in a study. Using a lengthy list of events that could happen to cardiac patients—such as chest pains, pneumonia, infection and death—Harris concluded that the group receiving prayers fared 11 percent better than the group that didn't, a number considered statistically significant.[40]

Of course, I don't need this study or any others to tell

THE LORD'S PRAYER: OUR GUIDE
" In this manner, therefore, pray:
Our Father in heaven,
Hallowed be Your name.
Your kingdom come.
Your will be done
On earth as it is in heaven.
Give us this day our daily bread.
And forgive us our debts, as we forgive our debtors.
And do not lead us into temptation,
But deliver us from the evil one.
For Yours is the kingdom and the power and
the glory forever. Amen."

—Matthew 6:9-13, NKJV

me what I know from personal experience. PRAYER IS POWERFUL!

I am convinced that intercessory prayer is the reason I am here today.

∾

I want to share a few principles I learned from the many prayer partners in my life about effective prayers, using The Lord's Prayer as a guide.

Make it personal! Praying out of rote and ritual can be an easy trap for all of us. Jesus warned against "babbling" nonsense when we pray.[41]

God wants a personal relationship with us and wants us to approach Him with familiarity, honesty and security like we would a father—"Our Father in heaven."

Max Lucado wrote: "Think of prayer less as an *activity for* God and more as an *awareness of* God. Seek to live in uninterrupted awareness. Acknowledge His presence everywhere you go. As you stand in line to register your car, think, Thank you, Lord, for being here. In the grocery as you shop, Your presence, my King, I welcome. As you wash the dishes, worship your Maker."[42]

Otis Ledbetter is a lifelong friend. He and I grew up together in east Texas. Our dads were both pastors which gave us plenty of opportunity to get into trouble.

In his book, *In the Secret Place,* he says, "I believe from God's Word that He has provided a secret place for each of His children to dwell with Him, a place He uniquely designed for each one in order to communicate His will to them. It isn't something only for the spiritual *haves*, to the exclusion of the *have-nots* (a demeaning distinction I don't believe in). God has a secret place waiting for you and for every believer—and the choice whether to meet Him there is entirely our own. No one knows your needs better than your Father in heaven. When He created you, He knew you would need a private place to meet Him—a place where no one else may enter, a path where only you and He can stroll. He calls it 'the secret place' (not just 'a' secret place) because there's only one like it for each of us."[43]

It's very important that each of us find our own secret place to meet God. Because of Jesus, we can have a more intimate, personal relationship with the Creator of the Universe through prayer and Scriptures. That's amazing!

Show Gratitude and Thanksgiving. According to Jesus' model prayer, after approaching our Heavenly Father, we are to offer worship and praise. "Our Father in heaven, Hallowed be Your name. Your kingdom come. Your will be done ..." When we acknowledge that God is all-powerful and in control, we infuse power into our prayer.

When Jesus performed the miracle of raising Lazarus from the dead, the first words He uttered in His prayer to His Father were of thanksgiving![44]

Expressing gratitude in times of anxiety and frustration has the incredible power to bring peace and comfort to you immediately.[45]

Now, I want you to understand that God doesn't command us to be thankful "for" everything, just to be thankful "in" everything. In the midst of my own pain and emotional distress, it would have been pushing it for me to say, "I thank you God for giving me cancer!" I wasn't feeling it. But eventually, I did come to that place.

It was possible for me to give thanks for the support of my friends and family ... for other blessings in my life ... and for God's presence and comfort during those difficult times.

In The Lord's Prayer, Jesus acknowledges God's daily provision—"Give us this day our daily bread."

Being thankful for all that God has already done in your life not only gets God's attention, but it gives you confidence. I try to keep in mind that no matter what I face today, God has already brought me through some tough times. I try to remain thankful for what He has done in my life ... what He has given me ... and what He is going to make happen for me.

Come with an Attitude of Repentance. "And forgive us our debts, as we forgive our debtors." We must remember to take inventory of our lives when we approach God in prayer. Remember, sometimes the storms we face are of our own doing—consequences of sin and bad decisions. God is full of grace and forgiveness *if* we ask for it.

Make a Petition. As Jesus was teaching the disciples how to pray, He was sure to include specific requests of God, including petitions for provision, forgiveness, strength from temptation and deliverance from the *"evil one."*

Paul also had specific requests when he prayed. He asked for God's guidance in spreading the Gospel and to be delivered from "evil men" among other things.[46] Jesus said if you want something, ask for it![47]

God wants to answer our prayers. He wants good things for His children.[48]

Leave it with God. Jesus ended The Lord's Prayer with a simple phrase that acknowledged His confidence and trust in God's control. "For Yours is the kingdom and the power and the glory forever. Amen."

I've said it before and I'll say it again. We may not understand the purpose of our trial. We may not know how it will all end. But one thing we can take to the bank—God does. He is Lord of all. He is in control. When you lay your troubles at His feet, you can walk away with assurance that you have set the wheels of faith into motion.

LIFE LESSONS LEARNED

The Power of Prayer

Prayer is a gift from God. Open lines of communication between you and your Heavenly Father are a blessing. Make a commitment to take advantage of this privilege through regular prayer.

For the most effective prayer, have an attitude of thankfulness, repentance and expectancy.

Don't be afraid to ask friends and family for prayer. Intercession is an incredible spiritual weapon. Don't let your pride get in the way of this reservoir of power!

5

VIA DOLOROSA

Finding Strength in the Lord

"God is our refuge and strength, an ever-present help in trouble. Therefore we will not fear."

—Psalm 46:1-2

Midway through my battle with cancer—struggling to keep my head above water and barely able to take it one day at a time—I admitted that I was not doing well.

My wife suggested that we get out of the house and do something as a family. She got all of us tickets for a university concert. I was so weak and tired that I tried to get out of it. We went anyway.

My long-time friend, Cal Thomas, a syndicated columnist and regular guest on Fox News, stood next to us as we waited to enter the concert. Cal politely asked me how I was feeling. Whether he expected an honest answer or not, he got one!

He tried to encourage me. "Vernon," he said, "I pray for you every day. Sometimes that is a cliché we use and it's not always true, but I really do."

Cal reached into his pocket, pulled out his day calendar and flipped it to the back. He showed me his prayer list and pointed to my name. It was at the top of his list. Then he put his hand on my shoulder and prayed for me right there as we waited in line.

There were more than 3,000 people there that night to hear the popular Christian singer, Sandi Patti. When we sat in our seats for the concert, Cal and his wife, Rae, were just two rows in front of me and my family. He was sitting on the aisle and so was I.

The lights dimmed, the concert started, and a wave of loneliness hit me head on, as if life was passing me by. I remember thinking, "No one understands what I'm feeling; no one understands what I'm going through." I was paralyzed with fear and a sense of utter loneliness.

Then, of all things, Sandi sang a song in Spanish. The verse in English grabbed my heart: "Down the Via Dolorosa—called the way of suffering, Like a lamb came the Messiah, Christ the King."

It suddenly dawned on me that there is someone who fully understood what I felt—someone who understood what I faced. Jesus knew what it was like to face death. He prayed, "Father if You are willing, take this cup from me."[49]

I was comforted. Jesus not only knew what I was going

JOURNAL ENTRY:

God, I'm so weak and I want to quit. Please help me find the strength to make it through this day.

through, He went through it all Himself. Because He understood, I could turn to Him and trust Him for strength and wisdom, even when I was lonely and didn't feel well.

Then something unexplainable happened in the middle of the song. Cal, who is tall, distinguished, and was wearing a suit and tie, got out of his seat, came to where I was sitting, sat down on the floor, crossed his legs, put his arm around me, and held my hand. He never said a word—he just held me.

It was more than I could bear! I cried, my wife cried, my children cried ... even the people behind us cried. It was such a touching and tender moment. It was as if Jesus had tapped Cal on the shoulder and said, "Cal, my friend, Vernon is not doing too well. Would you go back there and put your arms around him, comfort him and let him know that we care?"

It wasn't just Cal hugging me that night. Jesus was hugging me, too.

❧

It's OK to feel weak and discouraged. We don't have to rely on our own strength, because just when we sink to our lowest, God is there.

He sends encouragement our way in small and big moments.

One morning, I was home lying in bed, too weak and sick to get up. The phone rang and Patty said, "Vernon you need to speak to this person." Reluctantly, I picked up the

" One with God is a majority." —Billy Graham[50]

receiver and the person on the other end said, "Hey Vernon, this is Doug Oldham." Doug is one of my heroes. He is one of the giants of Gospel music and occasionally I would travel with him to his concerts, help set up his equipment and sell his records. I would always request that he sing my favorite song, "The King is Coming." Man ... can he sing!

Doug had just survived his own battle with cancer and out of the blue he was calling me. "I wanted to encourage you Vernon ... don't give up ... hang in there!" For over an hour we talked. I must have asked him a hundred questions—"What was it like? How did you feel? What did you do?" He patiently answered each one. I found unusual strength and encouragement from someone who had been there ... done that! It was a simple gesture, but his phone call was just the medicine I needed that day.

God knows what we face ... nothing catches Him by surprise. And no matter the severity of our storm, He will be there when we need Him ... when we call on Him! And He has promised to strengthen us.[51]

When life has ravaged my strength, I try to remember that God is in control. We may struggle, strive and manipulate. But in the final analysis, God knows what He is doing and will accomplish His purposes.[52]

In my own life, He has opened doors for ministry all over the world. I take comfort in that.

Behind the Bamboo Curtain of Communist China, Lin Xiangao, who also uses the Western name Samuel Lamb, spent over 20 years in prison for his evangelistic activities. He rose above his circumstances and is one of the most inspirational men I know! I'll never forget the day I first met this great man.

As I stepped into the taxi, I pulled a crumpled sheet of paper out of my pocket. On the paper was written an address in both English and Cantonese: 35 Da Ma Zhan.

In Guangzhou, a city of more than 3 million people, I had no idea where I was going and I was alone. My goal was to meet one of China's well-known house church leaders, Pastor Samuel Lamb.

When the Chinese taxi driver stopped in the middle of the street, I said, "No, no," and once again pointed to the small sheet of paper. He shook his head "yes" and pointed me in the direction of a small alley, barely 20 feet wide. "Da Ma Zhan," he said. It was nearly dark outside and the alley was packed with people. Families sat outside their doorways, mothers cooked rice, and older men—wearing their blue Mao jackets—played Mah-jongg, a Chinese game that looked a lot like Dominos to me. The smells of fish, steamed rice and vegetables filled the air. I definitely had stepped back in time.

Walking alone, I felt a little intimidated, but I had come too far to let fear stop me. I arrived at number 35—a small three-story apartment building—and as I expected, uniformed armed guards met me. They occupied the first floor, guarding Pastor Lamb who was under house arrest. He has endured more than 21 years in prison for his faith and because he refused to register his church with the Chinese government. Fifteen of those years, he did hard physical labor in a coal mine after he tried to make a copy of the New Testament.

While the pastor was in prison, his wife died, but the authorities never bothered to give him the news. After his eventual release, he returned to his apartment and learned of her death. Eleven months later, his mother—who was also living in their home—passed away.

I was eager to meet Pastor Lamb. His house church meeting had just dismissed, so I had to wait outside while hundreds of Chinese believers made their way down the narrow staircase and filed past me into the night. I'll never know how that many people fit inside that apartment. I had to push past the guards to make my way up the stairs. When I reached the third floor, I met my hero for the first time.

Pastor Lamb was short—I towered over him. With a contagious smile, he invited me to come in. The first thing I remember seeing was a long table with about 20 Chinese young people writing feverishly. Nearly 80 percent of the pastor's congregation are young people who are hungry for the Word of God and eager to share it with their friends.

I asked Pastor Lamb what they were doing. He matter-of-factly explained, "They are making handwritten copies of the Gospel of John to give to their friends at school tomorrow. We only have one Bible at this time, so we must make copies."

I thought to myself, "This would never happen in my country. Most Christian young people in America would never think of giving a Gospel of John to their friends in school, let alone make a handwritten copy."

As I sat there with this leader of the house church movement, he told me his stories and showed me his photos and an official Oval Office pen from Ronald Reagan. He told me that it was a gift from a White House staff member who told him, "President Reagan asked me to tell you to pray for him whenever you use this pen."

Pastor Lamb also showed me a photo of Billy Graham standing behind the makeshift pulpit in that Da Ma Zhan apartment.

As I looked around the apartment, I noticed that the walls were knocked out and replaced with wooden benches. In the far corner was a single bed, a small refrigerator and a hot plate—Pastor Lamb's living space. Every single inch of the rest of the apartment was converted to a meeting room for the Da Ma Zhan Church.

Pastor Lamb said that he started preaching again when he was released from prison and his house church started growing. One day, concerned authorities stormed into the meeting and arrested Pastor Lamb again. They confiscated all of the Bibles and hymnals. For three days, he was interrogated, beaten, and tortured. He was told to go back and close the Da Ma Zhan house church. I asked him, "What did you do?"

"I stood in the church the next week," he said, "and told the congregation that the police said not to come back."

"What happened?" I asked.

"The next Sunday," he said, "our church attendance doubled. Jesus said, *'Upon this rock I will build my church and the gates of hell will not prevail against it.'*"[53]

At the time, Da Ma Zhan Church was one of the largest house churches in China. Every week, more than 1,500 believers packed into five services.

I asked Pastor Lamb, "How did you survive all of those years in prison?"

"I quoted Scripture that I had committed to memory and composed hymns to worship God," he said. His two favorite biblical passages were written from prison to the Christians at Philippi and to young Timothy:

"Do not be anxious about anything, but in everything, by prayer and petition, with thanksgiving, present your requests to God. And the peace of God, which transcends all understanding, will guard your hearts and minds in Christ Jesus."[54]

"I have fought the good fight, I have finished the race, I have kept the faith. Now there is in store for me the crown of righteousness, which the Lord, the righteous Judge, will award to me on that day – and not only to me, but also to all who have longed for His appearing."[55]

"Pray for us dearly, because we don't know about tomorrow," Pastor Lamb said. "We don't know when tribulation will come. Pray that our people might have strength to face persecution. They are threatened by the government with no salary or no job if they attend the meetings, yet they still come. But please do not pray for the persecution to stop."

He saw his trial as a blessing, because every time they arrested him and sent him to prison, the church grew.

I asked Pastor Lamb how I could help him. He asked me to bring them more Bibles. Over the years, I have visited him many times, each time bringing him a load of Bibles—sometimes sending them ahead in vans, and sometimes not even telling him their source.

Every time I visited that special house church, I looked around and saw only a few Bibles. People crowded around and peered over the shoulders of those who held the Bibles, just to follow along as the Word of God was read aloud.

On many occasions, I saw people holding crumpled, torn pieces of paper. I soon realized these were pages torn from a Bible and shared in the group. This was not done out of disrespect for God's Word, but for the unquenchable desire to have a small portion of their very own.

On one of my visits, Pastor Lamb said the Public Security Bureau—the secret police—questioned him about my visit. They asked, "Why are you meeting with foreigners?"

"I am not," he said. "He is my brother."

One of the highlights of my life was one Sunday when Pastor Lamb invited me to speak to the Da Ma Zhan house church. He was my interpreter. What a memory!

∽

I am blessed to call Pastor Lamb my friend. He has endured more persecution than anyone I know. He was beaten and tortured for his faith—and his faith never wavered. Every time I am with him, he has a smile on his face and a song in his heart. He is God's gift to the underground church in China.

I learned so much about the power of faith from my friend at 35 Da Ma Zhan. Samuel Lamb may be small in stature, but he is a giant of the faith to me.

One of the things Pastor Lamb has taught me is to live life one day at a time. In your weak moments, you may have to just put one foot in front of the other and go one step at a time. You can *expect* discouragement, but just don't *accept* it.

When you do your best in every situation, you will find the strength and faith you need. Faith is like a muscle; when you exercise it in the small things, it will grow. One who lives their life to the best of their ability every day is someone who lives without regrets.

In 1904, a young man graduated from high school in Chicago, Illinois. He was a member of the Moody Bible Church. His name was William Borden, heir to the Borden Dairy Estate and a millionaire.

For a graduation gift, his parents sent him on an around-the-world cruise. He went to Hong Kong, through

"There are two kinds of people: those who say to God, 'Thy will be done,' and those to whom God says, 'All right, then, have it your way.'"

—*C.S. Lewis*[56]

Asia, Egypt, the Middle East and throughout the capitals of Europe. In each letter home to his parents, he graphically described his compassion and his burden as he saw the needs of thousands and millions of hurting people. In one letter he said, "Mom, I believe God is calling me to be a missionary." In another letter, he said, "I'm sure God is calling me. I'm going to give my life and prepare for the mission field."

He came home and spent four years at Yale University. The temptation was to forget his education and go straight into the mission field, but he said, "I want to be as prepared as possible." After that he spent three years at Princeton Seminary. While he was in college he had anonymously given away over $70,000 to the cause of missions here and there.

The story is told that when he prepared to go to the mission field he wrote two words in the back of his Bible— "**no reserves**." He learned to live by faith, to trust God for His power, for His might. There are no reserves in the Christian life.

One of the most encouraging chapters in the Bible was written by a man who suffered great tragedy and great triumph in life—David. "For troubles without number surround me; my sins have overtaken me, and I cannot see. They are more than the hairs of my head, and my heart fails within me" (Psalms 40:12). But whether he was on top of the world as a great king, or in deep tribulation as a sinner, God was never far away.

PSALM 23
A psalm of David.

The LORD is my shepherd, I shall not be in want.
He makes me lie down in green pastures, he leads me beside quiet waters, he restores my soul. He guides me in paths of righteousness for his name's sake.

Even though I walk through the valley of the shadow of death, I will fear no evil, for you are with me; your rod and your staff, they comfort me.

You prepare a table before me in the presence of my enemies. You anoint my head with oil; my cup overflows.

Surely goodness and love will follow me all the days of my life, and I will dwell in the house of the LORD forever.

He was offered many outstanding jobs upon graduation. He turned them all down, and he wrote two more words in the back of his Bible—**"no retreats."** He said, "God has called me, and I'm going."

He sailed for China to work with a small group of Muslims in that country. He stopped off in Egypt to do some preparation. While he was there he contracted cerebral meningitis and was dead within a month. You say, "What a waste. All that time preparing—what a waste!"

But he had written in the back of his Bible, underneath the words "no reserves," "no retreats," the two words—**"no regrets."**[57] And when the news of his death reached America, it was a front page story in every newspaper. As a result, thousands of American college students committed their lives to take his place. A great missionary movement was born!

౮

Strength to endure the storms of life can come from many places—friends, family, hope for good news, but the most powerful sustenance for your heart, mind and soul can only be found in the loving arms of God.

He loves you, my friend. He wants what is ultimately best for you and will never leave you. Trust in Him.

LIFE LESSONS LEARNED

Finding Strength in the Lord

God's grace and love can manifest itself anywhere. Be encouraged by hugs and prayers from friends and inspirational messages or songs. God can use them to send you a word or gesture of comfort and hope.

Take Him at His Word. When you are all alone and need some immediate encouragement, pick up your Bible. The promises of Scripture are true … you can rely on God to fulfill on His commitments to you.

Remember, you are never alone. Even on your weakest days, God is with you. He will never forsake you but longs to gather you under His wings of protection.

6

NOT ABOUT ME

Looking Past Our Trials

"My old self has been crucified with Christ. It is no longer I who live, but Christ lives in me."

—Galatians 2:20 NLT

O ne of the most surprising and liberating moments of my battle with cancer appropriately came on the Fourth of July.

We had received an invitation to a block party. About 20 families were planning on gathering with lawn chairs and barbecue grills in a cul de sac in the middle of our neighborhood. My wife asked what I wanted to do and I decided we should go.

So, here I was sitting in a lawn chair in the middle of the street surrounded by about 100 acquaintances enjoying the festivities. There was a steady roar of noise from laughter and discussion. My next-door neighbor walked over to chat. She had a patch on her eye following surgery and asked me how I had managed to cope with surgery and chemotherapy.

Here was an opportunity! Not all my neighbors had heard so I pretended like my hearing was affected too (everything else was) and asked her to repeat the question a little louder. When she did, everyone fell silent.

All eyes were on me. God gave me a platform to share my faith. I told them all how I could not have coped apart from my faith in God and relationship with Jesus Christ. Afterwards, I realized that in just five minutes, I had been able to share the Gospel with 100 people, many of whom would have never listened under any other circumstances.

It wasn't about me! It was about them! My struggle had provided the opportunity to share eternal hope.

The following day, another neighbor was working in his yard and motioned me over. He still had a lot of unanswered questions about salvation. I tried to answer them as best I could. We continued to have conversations about faith often.

Even though it was a painful journey, God had a plan to use my situation to reach my neighbors. When I caught a glimpse of that purpose, it was indescribable.

The fact that the impact of my trial can go beyond my own selfish little circle of life continues to amaze me.

I got a call one day from one of our generous ministry supporters who told me that the mayor of Lynchburg had lost his voice because of cancer and was really depressed. She asked if I could call or visit him because I had gone through similar circumstances.

I did and when we talked in his office, the mayor asked lots of questions! We prayed together and met several more times for prayer and to talk. Today, this man is an elder in church and one of the strongest supporters of our ministry. We have a deep relationship that was forged in our mutual journey of pain. It wasn't about me! It was about a man in pain and being the tool God used to comfort him.

Through these encounters, I began to realize that there was a purpose beyond my pain and that my journey wasn't just about me. It was a liberating realization that has impacted my life ever since and changed the way I view challenges and trials.

∽

To be perfectly honest, in the midst of my struggle I admit that I was, at times … well, selfish and self-centered. But in a fight for your life sometimes you don't have a choice.

There were times when every ounce of my strength and sanity were focused on just surviving … getting through the day … enduring the next round of tests … holding my emotions together through bad news. Part of the basic instinct for survival that we all have is pulling in and pre-serving ourselves when we feel threatened. But sometimes the selfish attitude can get out of hand.

I had days where I was so consumed with my own pain that I could not see past my own selfish needs. Lucky for me I had an incredible support group of family and friends who knew when to let me be, when to handle me with kid gloves, and when to set me straight.

One day, my wife told me to quit feeling sorry for myself. "You're not the only person in the world suffering. Get up and let's go about life," she said. And she was right.

"God loves you right where you are but he doesn't want to leave you there."

—Max Lucado[58]

One of the most refreshing, hopeful moments you experience in your trial can be when something happens that makes you sit back and think, "Hmmm. It's not all about me."

We all have a purpose for our lives.[59] God commands us to reach out to others, not stay within ourselves. But we must go through preparation to achieve God's plans. Our storms of life have a purpose that is greater than us. They are part of the preparation God has for our lives. Our trials give us maturity and completion so that we can impact the lives of others![60]

An inspiring pastor and author of a generation ago once said, "Those who have endured the stinging experiences are the choicest people God can use. Who God would use greatly, He will hurt deeply."[61]

Someone else once said, "Many people owe the grandeur of their lives to their tremendous trials."[62]

Stormy times, whether we like them or not, force us to grow up real quick spiritually and mature in Christ. They give us greater understanding and confidence. Trials shape and mold us, test us in fire, and make us complete for God's purposes.

JOURNAL ENTRY:

Father, I am amazed at how You are opening doors for me to share my story and faith! I don't thank You enough ...

Everything we go through ... every trial we face helps prepare us and make us more effective in our calling.

Corrie Ten Boom's story is one of the most incredible examples of how struggles can mature us and equip us to impact the lives of many others.

Corrie and her family were watchmakers who lived in Holland during World War II. The family hid Jews in their home and helped many escape death at the hands of the Nazis ... until the entire family was arrested on February 28, 1944. They were sent first to Scheveningen concentration camp, then to the Vught political concentration camp (both in the Netherlands), and finally to Ravensbruck concentration camp in Germany in September 1944, where Corrie's sister Betsie died.[63]

Though she didn't know it at the time, the concentration camp was the fire that molded Corrie for a higher calling. There she learned how to cling to her faith and trust in God ... no matter what the consequences. She wrote:

"The school of life offers some difficult courses, but it

is in the difficult class that one learns the most—especially when your teacher is the Lord Jesus Christ.

"God has plans—not problems—for our lives. Before she died in the concentration camp in Ravensbruck, my sister Betsie said to me, 'Corrie, your whole life has been a training for the work you are doing here in prison—and for the work you will do afterward.'

"Looking back across the years of my life, I can see the working of a divine pattern which is the way of God with His children. In the German camp, with all its horror, I found many prisoners who had never heard of Jesus Christ. Many died, or were killed, but many died with the name of Jesus on their lips. They were well worth all our

JOURNAL ENTRY:

God, I want to see the world with Your eyes. There are so many people in pain. I ask You to send peace and hope to others who are suffering from disease, heartbreak, fear and personal battles.

Will You help me see past my own problems to others who are hurting? Equip me to impact the lives of others as You have called me to do.

Shine Your light through me! Amen.

"It's odd that you can get so anesthetized by your own pain or your own problem that you don't quite fully share the hell of someone close to you."

—Lady Bird Johnson[64]

suffering. Faith is like radar which sees through the fog—the reality of things at a distance that the human eye cannot see."[65]

On December 28, 1944, after 10 months of incarceration in concentration camps, Corrie Ten Boom was set free. She later learned that it was an error in paperwork that caused her to be released from prison and that all the women prisoners her age and older were killed at the end of that very week.[66]

For the next four decades following her release from prison, Corrie traveled extensively, speaking in more than 60 countries, captivating audiences with her inspiring faith and love for God. She is the author of nine books, one of which is *The Hiding Place*, a personal account of her arrest and time spent in prison. She also produced five films.

Her life story gives us all hope and assurance that we can look past our trials and use our experiences to make a real difference for others. My prayer is that God will use me … that He will allow me to accomplish things that will live beyond my own life.

If you feel like you have been consumed in the fires of a trial in your life … or like you are being crushed by its pressures, take heart. Good things will come to you as you persevere![67]

God is molding and shaping you for a greater purpose than you can even imagine. Cling to your faith. Make it your refuge and hiding place. When you come through the fire, you will be mature, whole and complete—ready to impact the lives of others.

Remember, your struggle is not just about you, it's about sharing the hope and love of Jesus Christ with others. Be encouraged that God is preparing you for incredible things!

LIFE LESSONS LEARNED

Looking Past Our Trials

Face your trials with determination. Perseverance is the key to finding the maturity and benefits of our struggles in life.

Look around and notice what others are going through. Maybe God has given you a special insight or sensitivity to the needs of others because of your experiences. Allow Him to use you to comfort others.

Take advantage of every opportunity God gives you.

Share your faith and hope with every person you can. Maybe the nurse in the chemotherapy unit needs to hear about God's love today and you are her only light.

7

BOLL WEEVIL

Lessons Learned

"For I consider that the sufferings of this present time are not worthy to be compared with the glory which shall be revealed in us."

—Romans 8:18, NKJV

I was visiting one of my good friends, Gary Aldridge, who pastors a church in Montgomery, Alabama. He must have thought I was crazy when I asked him to take me to the town of Enterprise. He said, "Vernon, that's a two-hour drive from Montgomery, and there's nothing there! It's just a small town." I told him, "I really need to go."

We spent the morning driving to Enterprise, and when we pulled into that little town, population just over 22,000, there it was—right in the middle of Main Street—a statue of a boll weevil! It was kind of ugly, but it was there.

I asked Gary to stop the car. We got out and I handed him my camera. I asked him to take my picture standing in front of the statue. He snapped the photo, we got back in the car and drove two hours back to Montgomery.

Enterprise, Alabama, is a town where cotton used to be king. In fact, cotton was the only crop grown there; the town depended on it until tragedy struck. One year, there was an attack of boll weevils that wiped out the entire cotton crop. The town was devastated.

They didn't know what they were going to do. But, instead of dwelling in discouragement and living in defeat, one farmer said, "We'll just grow peanuts instead." He went out and planted a peanut crop, and another farmer followed, and then another, until all the farmers did the same thing—they all planted peanuts.

That year, the town had a bumper crop. They made more money selling peanuts than they had ever made with cotton. Afterwards, one of the farmers was so grateful, he put up a monument to the boll weevil in the center of town.

The townspeople saw the benefit in their ordeal.

They accepted the fact that circumstances that seem so devastating can actually change our lives for good. In other words, they erected a monument to their crisis.

I liked that idea so much that I did the same thing. I decided to erect a monument to cancer in my life. I knew immediately what that monument would be—something to represent an irreplaceable benefit that came of my own crisis.

Years before, as a young high school student growing up in a pastor's home, I rebelled.

I rebelled against God ... against my parents' authority ... against the rules of strict Christianity that didn't make any sense to me. My walk with God became non-existent. I began to do things that a Christian shouldn't do—especially one living in a pastor's home—and I ran

In gratitude for lessons taught, residents erected the world's only monument to an agricultural pest, the boll weevil. The base of the monument is inscribed: "In profound appreciation of the boll weevil and what it has done as the herald of prosperity. This monument was erected by the citizens of Enterprise, Coffee County, Alabama."[68]

from God. My dad and I argued and fought on a regular basis. It wasn't a pretty sight!

One day, with $25 in my pocket and one small suitcase, I stood in the front yard of our home, clenched my fist, shook it in my dad's face, and said, "I don't care if I ever see you again."

As a 19-year-old college student, I left home. Through the years, I came back to God, but my relationship with my father was still strained. We would spend the perfunctory times of Christmas and Thanksgiving together, but there was no deep relationship ... not until I had cancer.

One day, I realized that I was the cause of our fractured relationship. I remember going to my dad and saying, "Do you remember that day in the front yard?" He said, "Yes."

Looking him in the eye, I said, "For that day and every day just like it, I want you to know I was so wrong. I know

I hurt you deeply and I'm asking you to please forgive me."

My dad did something that I never recall him doing before—he embraced me. He began to weep uncontrollably and kept saying over and over, "I love you."

To this day, we never end a conversation or a phone call without saying to each other, "I love you."

The night before my first surgery for cancer, my father, who lived five hours away, drove through the night to be with me during that operation. He made the trip 17 more times and was by my side during every single surgery. A few days after my first operation, he sent me a tear-stained, handwritten letter that I treasure.

So, I knew what my monument would be. I had the letter matted and framed, and it hangs in my office where I can see it every day.

This letter is my monument to cancer ... it's better than a statue of a boll weevil any day!

If nothing else but a deeper, truer relationship with my dad had come of my battle with cancer, I would have been grateful. It is a gift that may have never happened if it were not for this crisis.

Through my battle with cancer, I have gained:

The faith to believe God in impossible situations. When God wants to show us His power, He has to start with a difficulty. You cannot have a miracle without an impossibility. God gave me the peace and assurance that He was not finished with my life and that He has the power to accomplish His purpose.

Just like Andrae Crouch's Gospel song, "Through it All,"

Dear Vernon,

In these past two weeks, there has been much searching and struggle for me.

My heart is broken because of your pain and affliction; even now while I am writing, I cannot hold back the tears. I have cried enough tears for the both of us, walking the floor and weeping through the night.

It has not been as difficult for me to accept the fact of your having Hodgkin's, but I am having a hard time accepting the injury to your voice and your vocal cords. Yet I know that God doesn't make any mistakes, and that He is still in control, and that Romans 8:28 is still true. However, I know what it means to think thoughts and feel feelings, and not be able to express them, and it hurts me deeply to think that this could happen to you.

Would to God that I could bear this pain and affliction for you; it would be much easier for me to do. But that would rob you of God's blessed purpose for you, and the blessing that He is going to build in you, and the way that He is going to use you with whatever voice He gives you.

In your personal odyssey of catastrophe, I pray there will be this absorbing thought: God knows and feels your pain just as He did at the grave of Lazarus, and He weeps for you. Please take comfort knowing that His comfort is not insulations from the difficulty; but rather it is spiritual fortification, sufficient to enable you to stand firm, undefeated in this fiery trial God is permitting you to bear (2 Corinthians 1:4).

I just want you to know that I am bearing this with you... and I love you, and I have never loved you more.

—Dad

P.S. This is Friday — but Sunday is coming!

"Failures are finger posts on the road to achievement."

—*C.S. Lewis*[69]

I've learned to trust in God and actually be thankful for my storm. Without my trials and struggles, I would never have known the comfort and power that can be found in the loving arms of God.

A new commitment to the importance of prayer. I realize that God does answer prayer. Now I understand the power of prayer and have a renewed passion and dedication to incorporating prayer into my daily life.

A deeper appreciation for my family and friends. My wife, children and my parents are so much more valuable to me. The grief of thinking I would never see my children grow up has allowed me to savor every moment of their lives. I take time to spend with my children and grandchildren. I look at life as a wonderful gift to be enjoyed! Also, some of my dearest friendships in life were forged in the fires of cancer. I'm grateful for those who wept with me and prayed with me. They are my soul mates.

A platform to minister to others. My suffering has opened more doors and ears to the Gospel than I ever dreamed possible! Consider how your trial will gain you an audience to share the hope of Jesus Christ.

"Faith is taking the first step even when you don't see the whole staircase."

—*Martin Luther King Jr.*[70]

THROUGH IT ALL
Words and music by Andrae Crouch

I've had many tears and sorrows
I've had questions for tomorrow
There've been times I didn't know right from wrong
But in every situation
God gave blessed consolation
That my trials only come to make me strong

I've been a lot of places
And I've seen so many faces
But there've been times I've felt so all alone
But in that lonely hour
In that precious, lonely hour
Jesus let me know I was His own

So I thank God for the mountains
And I thank Him for the valleys

I thank Him for the storms He's brought me through
Cause if I never had a problem
I wouldn't know that He could solve them
I wouldn't know what faith in His Word could do

Through it all
Through it all
I've learned to trust in Jesus
I've learned to trust in God
Through it all
Through it all
I've learned to depend upon His Word
Yes, I've learned to depend upon His Word
I've learned to depend upon His Word[71]

⁓

For nearly two years, I could not speak in public. It was one of the most frustrating aspects of my ordeal. When the doctors injected the Teflon into my vocal cords ... it gave me hope.

Jerry Falwell knew that it was important for me to "get back in the saddle" as soon as possible. So one Sunday he announced that I would be speaking for 10 minutes in the evening service. He didn't want my first time back to be physically taxing, so he said, "Vernon, you speak for 10 minutes and then I'll preach and give an invitation."

That night, the church was packed. It was the weekend of Liberty University's graduation. Hundreds of parents, relatives and friends were there. I sat on the platform and looked into the faces of thousands of students who had prayed for me. Many of my pastor friends that had prayed for me for two years were there as well, and all my family— it was a big moment.

When I stood to speak my legs were weak, but for the first time in nearly two years, my voice was strong. I simply shared what God had taught me in my battle with cancer. And after 10 minutes, I sat down. The silence was deafening; and then you could hear the sounds of weeping.

Jerry stood and said, "We have already heard from God tonight; we don't need another sermon." More people began to weep. Quietly, spontaneously, one by one, people began to get out of their seats ... some knelt at the altar to pray, some went to one another to pray. It was a very unusual "moving" of the Holy Spirit. After a few minutes, Jerry's son, Jonathan, who was sitting in the back of the sanctuary, walked down that long aisle, from the back to the front.

JOURNAL ENTRY.

No sense worrying about yesterday. It's already gone. No sense worrying about tomorrow. It may never come. I'm going to focus on today.

Jerry did something I had rarely seen him do. He left the pulpit in the middle of the invitation and walked down to meet his son. That night, Jonathan committed his life to ministry. I will never forget the sight of Jerry and Jonathan hugging one another, weeping openly and praying in front of the entire congregation. After a few moments, they left the sanctuary and went to the prayer room.

That night, I preached only 10 minutes, but that spontaneous moving of God lasted nearly an hour. Many people came to faith that night. Many Christians came back to God, and Jonathan Falwell gave his life to be a minister of the Gospel. Today, he is the Executive Pastor of Thomas Road Church, the spiritual leader of thousands.

On the way home that night, I was reflecting on how incredible God was, when out of the blue, my wife asked me, "What did you learn tonight?" I thought her question was kind of odd since this was my first message in two years. She continued, "You only preached 10 minutes, and look what God did. You need to remember … sometimes less is more."

God uses us in both big and small ways, but the impact is always incredible! Sometimes, we don't even know the full impact of our life's testimony.

My doctor told me during one of my office visits that he admired my faith. He might as well have rolled out the red carpet for me. "I appreciate you and have confidence in your medical skills," I told him. "But it's real important for you to know that I trust in God ultimately and if I survive, it will be God that will heal me." The doctor replied, "Don't lose that … that is what will get you through."

Sometimes the hard times in life are gifts in disguise … especially when they bring us closer to God.

LIFE LESSONS LEARNED

Lessons Learned

Depend on God daily. Whether you are in the midst of a storm or not, I want to challenge you to commit your day to God every single morning. Make a conscious effort to trust Him and believe Him for guidance every single day. It will make a big difference!

Focus on what really matters. Consider what is most important to you in life. Then decide not to waste your time and energy worrying about the small stuff.

Take note of how you feel differently about life. Is your family more valuable to you than ever before? Have you established a daily routine of prayer and Bible study? If so, keep these lessons close to your heart long after your storm is over.

8

DON'T TOUCH!

The Gift of Compassion

"Love one another. As I have loved you, so you must
love one another.

—John 13:34

"Wash your hands often, be careful what you eat,
what you touch, and remember your immune
system is compromised; just be careful."

After a nearly two-year battle with cancer, my immune
system was weak, which made me susceptible to colds, the
flu and every other illness. I still felt like life was passing me
by, and I had to make up for lost time.

At the time, I was Vice President of Liberty University,
and we were taking a team of faculty and students to Africa.

I had no idea what I was going to do; I just knew I had
to do something.

After much persuasion and arm-twisting, my doctors
reluctantly agreed to let me go ... but not without plenty of
warnings and shots.

There was a famine in Africa with thousands starving to
death in the Sudan and Ethiopia. The world was uniting to
do something to help, and I had been on the sidelines far
too long because of cancer. I was finally better and wanted
to do my part.

After arriving in Nairobi, Kenya, we chartered a small single-engine plane and flew north past the equator all the way to the Sudan border. We landed on a gravel runway. In the distance, I could see a village of grass huts. I had never seen a village like that before, except in National Geographic, of course, so I was intrigued.

As we got off the plane it was already over 100 degrees—we could feel the unbearable heat and humidity.

We were met by an African pastor, and I asked him whether we had time to visit the village and take some photos—that's what Americans do on the mission field. Because of the famine and drought, there was no fresh water anywhere. Large trucks had to bring water in every day from as far away as 80 kilometers. It was sobering to see tribal women on their knees, digging with their bare hands in dry riverbeds, trying to find water. The pastor said, "They won't find any water, but if they do, it will probably be contaminated and do them more harm than good." I had never seen anything like that before.

We arrived at the village of grass huts only to find it deserted—not a soul in sight. I began taking photos, snooping around and actually went up to one of the huts. It didn't have a door, only an opening with an animal-skin covering. I stuck my head in to look around and was surprised to see a little girl, maybe 9 years old, standing just inside in the doorway.

She startled me and I'm sure I startled her. All she was wearing was a dirty pair of underpants ... no shirt. She was filthy, her hair was matted, her nose was running and her belly was distended—showing the early signs of malnutrition. There were open running sores all over her body and the smell was awful. All I could think about was my doctor's parting words: "Be careful what you touch." I was so repulsed that I took a giant step backward and froze.

At that moment, God taught me a lesson that continues to shape my ministry. *He taught me about compassion.* I didn't hear any audible voices, but I did hear the Spirit of God quietly chasten me, "Wait just a minute. Who do you think you are? Do you see that little girl? I love that little girl just as much as I love your girls back home. I love that little girl so much, I sent my Son to die for her … and I have commanded you to love that little girl, too." Man, was I humbled and convicted.

Partly out of guilt and partly out of impulse, I reached forward and picked up that dirty, smelly little girl and held her tight in my arms. I later found out that I was the first white person she had ever seen, so I'm sure I scared her to death. I couldn't speak her language and she couldn't speak mine; all I could do was communicate with her in the international language of love. I held her … I touched her cheek … I tried my best to show her that I cared.

JOURNAL ENTRY:

Today my eyes were opened to true pain and suffering. I cannot believe how those poor families are forced to live!

"Jesus reached out His hand and touched the eyes of the blind, the skin of the person with leprosy and the legs of the cripple ... Jesus knew love usually involved touching."

—Dr. Paul Brand[72]

What happened next is still hard to believe after all these years. While I was holding that lonely and destitute little girl, out from the hut came her mother, her father, her brothers and sisters, and even her grandparents. I didn't realize that so many people could fit inside. Not only did the hut empty out, but within minutes I was surrounded by everyone in the village—several hundred starving and thirsty nomadic Turkana Africans.

I saw an elderly woman who was blind, a man with a tumor on his neck— obviously terminal, and another man whose leg had swollen three or four times its normal size. I looked into the eyes of the diseased, the blind and the lame. For the first time in my life, I realized what Jesus must have felt when he *"saw the crowds and was moved with compassion."*[73]

That day, in the middle of grass huts, God taught me compassion.

Most of us consider compassion as simply feeling sorry for someone or having a mild touch of pity for someone,

"Let my heart be broken with the things that break the heart of God."

—Robert Pierce

but the Bible defines compassion as much more than that.

In Matthew, when Jesus "was moved with compassion," it wasn't just pity; it literally was "suffering together with someone." That's what Jesus did. He suffered *with* them.

He held the children, He touched the lepers, He touched the blind man's eyes. When Jesus was confronted with great human need—death, disease, hunger and the plight of the homeless—He was "moved with compassion."

At the end of the Korean War, evangelist Billy Graham and Robert Pierce, the founder of World Vision and Samaritan's Purse, were faced with the dilemma of thousands of homeless orphaned children. Pierce made a statement that is now famous. "Let my heart be broken with the things that break the heart of God."[74]

That's my favorite definition of compassion.

I have a confession to make. I am not a compassionate person by nature; I am selfish. I don't wake up in the morning thinking about others. I think about me, my needs and my family.

(In fact, truth be known, when I wake up in the morning, I have only one overriding thought—"How quickly can I get caffeine into my system?" I am not even human until I have had a cup of coffee.)

Apart from the Spirit of God, I am not a compassionate person, so I find myself regularly, sometimes daily, praying, "Lord, let my heart be broken with the things that break Your heart."

Even though my battle with cancer has given me a greater sensitivity to the pain of others, I am still learning to feel the compassion of Christ.

∾

No matter what our own circumstances, God has called us to have compassion on others. Jesus is our example ...

He performed many miracles to meet the physical needs of desperate people—healing the blind, making the lame to walk and more.

He also had compassion on the hungry when He fed five thousand men, besides women and children with only five loaves of bread and two fish.[75] Not only is He concerned for our physical bodies, but also our spiritual well-being.[76]

Jesus knew His purpose on earth was to prepare souls for eternity through His teaching and sacrifice.[77]

His compassion did not end with empathy; He put His concern into action. Jesus did not just feel bad about the multitudes not having anything to eat; He did something about it. When He saw someone suffering physically, He healed them! And because of His compassion for our lost souls, He came to this earth to die and become a human

"For I was hungry and you gave me something to eat, I was thirsty and you gave me something to drink, I was a stranger and you invited me in, I needed clothes and you clothed me, I was sick and you looked after me, I was in prison and you came to visit me.'

Then the righteous will answer him, 'Lord, when did we see you hungry and feed you, or thirsty and give you something to drink? When did we see you a stranger and invite you in, or needing clothes and clothe you? When did we see you sick or in prison and go to visit you?' The King will reply, 'I tell you the truth, whatever you did for one of the least of these brothers of mine, you did for me.'"

—Matthew 25:35-40

sacrifice so that we might live! On earth, Jesus was a living, breathing example of God's compassion. He commands us to be the same.

If we love Jesus, He has instructed us to show our compassion for others in His name.[78]

⁓

"God has given us two hands, one to receive with and the other to give with."

—*Billy Graham*[79]

When we put hands and feet to our compassion, God helps us accomplish something lasting, fulfilling and eternal.

I can't help but remember the little girl in the village of grass huts. I felt so helpless in the face of such great human suffering and need. I asked my African pastor friend if he had anything that we could give them. He said he had a case of corn meal in the back of his vehicle. He willingly let me have it. We gave one small five-pound bag to each family. You would have thought it was Christmas morning … everyone was smiling and laughing. They thanked me, and some even hugged me. It left an indelible memory.

The African villagers told me their greatest need was water. They were dying! I shared words of encouragement and hope. And as the pastor interpreted, I also shared the good news of the Gospel. I told the pastor that we had to do something more, and I asked him to drive me to the district governmental offices. The officials described the crisis. They needed to drill wells immediately, if they were going to save lives. I didn't even know what it cost to drill a well, but the words were out of my mouth: "We will do it … by faith … we will do it."

When I returned to Liberty University, I shared the need and my experiences. I challenged students to do something bigger than themselves—to make a difference in someone else's life, to be moved with compassion. I wasn't prepared for their response. The money for the wells was raised in one week, and the life-giving water soon began to flow.

They gave their money, but they also gave their lives. Ten students stepped up and committed to taking a semester out of school to go to northern Kenya. They would oversee the drilling of the wells, establish a medical clinic and plant a church.

At the end of that semester, 10 more students took their place, and the next semester another 10, and then another 10. Three years later, the wells and the medical clinic had saved hundreds of lives, and the church had witnessed the salvation of many souls.

Everyone in that village of grass huts had become a Christ-follower during that three-year period, and my life and theirs would never be the same. Beyond that, hundreds of students did something that would last for eternity.

Part of what turns our trials into victories is our reaction. When we act out of love and compassion toward others, we can rise above our own situations.

Compassion is a gift from God that allows us to forget our own problems in the effort to help others.

LIFE LESSONS LEARNED

The Gift of Compassion

No matter what your situation in life, there is always someone else with greater suffering. Try to look past your own troubles and see what others are going through. It is a critical exercise that will give you growth and greater depth of emotion.

Make every effort to see the world through the eyes of Jesus. There are so many men, women and children who have needs, both physically and spiritually. Many will only come to know Jesus through the compassionate action of others.

Exercise your compassion muscles. Providing financial support to groups doing compassionate work is great, but if you are physically able, it is so rewarding to get your own hands dirty! Volunteer at a food bank, pass out clothes or food through your local Salvation Army branch, join church mission trips. Experience the joy of helping others! There is nothing like it!

9

A NEW BEGINNING

The Triumph of My Tragedy

"For I am about to do something new. See, I have already begun! Do you not see it?"

—Isaiah 43:19, NLT

When I began my journey with cancer, I had no idea where it would lead. I didn't even consider that God would have a completely new direction for my ministry and that His plan would lead me into the most fulfilling work of my entire life!

Once God had healed me of cancer and I had recovered from my medical crisis, I was ready to say, "OK God, I know you have a purpose and a plan for me. What do you want me to do with the rest of my life?"

I served six more years at Liberty University, taking students around the world on missions efforts. It was incredible. These were wonderful years of learning, sharing, and although I didn't know it at the time, establishing contacts and friends I would later need for the work God had in mind.

Then, when I least expected it, God began to move. Two Lynchburg businessmen, Jimmy Thomas and Dan Reber, took me to lunch. That conversation in a noisy, crowded restaurant changed the course of my life and has impacted millions of people around the world.

These two friends asked me if I would pray about helping them get Bibles into Russia, where Communism had just disintegrated. I agreed because I already had a network of partners in Eastern Block countries from my many trips with Liberty students.

In 1991, I accompanied Peter Deyneka on a trip to Moscow to meet Russian pastors and Christian leaders. He and his father had been exiled because of their faith and it was Peter's first trip back since he was a teenager. That divine appointment sparked a new evangelism calling for me and launched the beginnings of World Help—the ministry of God's design.

Early on, World Help distributed 500,000 Russian New Testaments on military bases and in public schools. We mailed 3 million copies of a 32-page booklet by a martyred born-again Russian orthodox priest murdered by the KGB—*To Be a Christian*—to every home in Moscow.

In these outreaches to Russia I found a new beginning, an incredible ministry opportunity and a deeper passion to touch lives than I had ever before experienced.

But it was also on one of my trips to Russia that, once again, I came face to face with my personal crisis—cancer.

☙

On a cold November day in Moscow, there was already more than two feet of snow on the ground. It was in the early months of the fall of Communism; everywhere I

"God is most glorified in us when we are most satisfied in Him."

—John Piper [80]

turned there was poverty, broken infrastructure, and lots pot holes in the roads. The majority of Russian men were drunk on Vodka by noon. They had nothing to live for and no hope for the future. The streets were dark, there were long lines for food, and all too often, the stores ran out of supplies before 10:00 a.m.

As I looked around, I saw nothing but blank looks on people's faces. They were depressing times.

I was invited to visit Cancer Hospital #62, the leading cancer institute in all of Russia, because we were Americans with the name "World Help." At first, I didn't want to go. As a cancer survivor, the thought of seeing terminally ill patients in a hopeless situation was depressing to me. My Russian host and interpreter said, "You must go. They are expecting you." Reluctantly, I agreed to the visit, but I was not happy about it.

When I got there, much to my surprise, nearly every patient in the hospital was waiting in the large meeting room to greet me. The room was crowded with doctors and nurses in long white gowns, some patients in wheel chairs, and others with walkers. Some were even rolled in on their beds. The only two patients in the entire hospital who were not there were in intensive care. There were more than 300 people in that meeting room.

I looked around at all the suffering cancer patients—waiting to die. They were not dying from cancer alone but from lack of adequate medical treatment they desperately needed. As a cancer survivor, this was almost too much to bear—too much to see. I was overwhelmed.

I remembered that I had several boxes of Russian/English parallel New Testaments in the vehicle outside. We gave each patient one as a gift. They were all so excited and for a brief moment, there were smiles. In a way, it was sad that they would be so happy over such a small gift.

Although it was difficult for me to be there that day, I could relate to the patients' suffering. I knew the pain they were feeling, and I understood the fear in their eyes. Hospital officials asked me to speak to the patients and share my faith.

"I am a cancer survivor," I said. Immediately, many people in the room began to weep.

Then I realized that there were probably very few cancer survivors at that time in Moscow. Even though they had wonderful doctors and nurses, their medical resources were almost non-existent. They had very little pain medication or chemotherapy; they didn't even have enough rubber gloves. The hospital paid two people each night to wash the gloves that were used that day so doctors and nurses could reuse them again in the morning.

I looked into the faces of men and women who would

be dead in a few months. It was sobering.

"Yes, I am a cancer survivor," I told them. "But someday I will die, and so will you. Today, I have come to tell you how you can live forever."

For the next 10-15 minutes, I shared my faith through an interpreter. More than 50 of the doctors, nurses and patients came to faith in Jesus Christ that day in Cancer Hospital #62.

After I spoke, hospital staff members took me on a tour of the hospital. This was an extremely emotional experience. I saw empty medicine cabinets and patients in recovery with no bandages to cover their wounds. Shocked, I witnessed a patient who had just received a tracheotomy. Because no surgical tubing was available, the doctors placed a used soda straw in his throat so he could breathe.

My first response was to turn and run from this frightening sight, but I knew God had sent me there to that hospital for a reason—to help these people.

Even though I could easily identify with them and their suffering, I could not relate to their lack of resources and lack of hope. These patients were in a top Russian medical facility, yet there were not enough supplies and medicines to effectively treat them. Basically, people were sent to this hospital to die.

Dr. Mahkson, the Chief Surgeon of the hospital, gave me a list of urgent needs—several pages long. He asked for my help. I looked at the list and had no idea where or how I could help, but I couldn't refuse him.

"I can't promise you how much I will be able to help,"

"God cannot give us a happiness and peace apart from Himself, because it is not there. There is no such thing."

—C.S. Lewis[81]

I said. "But I will promise you this ... I *will* help you."

Several weeks later, on my next visit to Moscow, I led a team with Joni Eareckson Tada and 66 of her friends. In the summer of 1967, Joni suffered a spinal cord fracture in a diving accident that left her paralyzed from the neck down. After two years of rehabilitation and newfound skills and determination, she has dedicated her life to helping others in similar situations. She has been an inspiration to millions as a speaker, author, and radio personality. Her story is an incredible example of triumph in tragedy!

Many of Joni's friends were physically disabled and in wheelchairs. We spent the entire week visiting hospitals, orphanages, and public schools, distributing Russian New Testaments. Joni presented her incredible testimony of overcoming suffering and finding hope in life. It was "magic."

Friday night in the Olympic village, several thousand people packed in to hear her, and hundreds came to faith in Christ that evening. On Monday night at dinner, one of Joni's friends rolled over to my table in his wheelchair and asked if we could talk. He told me he had a friend in

Tucson, Arizona, who had a warehouse full of medical supplies—just collecting dust.

"If I can get him to donate these to World Help," he asked me, "will you see that they get to Cancer Hospital #62?" I immediately agreed, and he was thrilled.

When he wheeled back to his table, I turned to my Russian host and asked him what he thought it would cost to ship a container of medical supplies from the United States to Moscow. He said it would cost at least $10,000.

My first thought was, "Dear God, what have I done?" But I realized that the same God who healed me from cancer was in control of this situation too. Little did I realize how much in control He was!

A few hours later, I attended the world famous Bolshoi Ballet with Joni and all 66 of her friends. I wasn't thrilled to be *there*. My idea of fun is watching 22 grown men with pads and helmets, not watching men tiptoe around in white tights pretending to be swans—no offense to people who like swans and the ballet.

I woke up at half time, which I am told they call "intermission." Much to my surprise, I recognized two U.S. Congressmen standing in the aisle, Congressmen Newt Gingrich of Georgia and Congressmen Dick Gephardt of Iowa. The Republican was standing on the right and the Democrat was standing on the left—I couldn't help but find that amusing!

Being the bashful soul that I am, I introduced myself to them. They asked me why I was in Moscow, and I told them about Joni and her friends and all the wonderful things God had done that week. They were genuinely interested. Then I asked them what *they* were doing in Moscow. They said, "We are here to finalize the details of the Russian American Aid Package."

The Berlin wall had just come down; Russia was now a fledgling democracy. I remember thinking, "Hmmm ... Russian American Aid Package ... Hmmm."

My brain shifted into high gear. "Congressmen," I said, "if I had a container of medical supplies that needed to be shipped from the United States to Cancer Hospital #62, could that be considered part of the Russian American Aid Package?" They both replied, "Yes, of course!" God was obviously working behind the scenes to fulfill His plan.

The Congressmen gave me the name of their liaison, and when I returned to the United States, we immediately went to work. Louanne Guillerman, whose husband Pierre was the President of Liberty University at the time, volunteered to travel to Tucson to inventory the medical supplies. She shipped them to our offices in Virginia.

It was a happy, memorable day when the National Guard came to our office, inspected the container, sealed it, and gave it official permission as a Russian American Aid Package. That first container was shipped, at no cost to World Help, to Cancer Hospital #62 in Moscow, Russia— our tax dollars at work!

I couldn't be in Moscow when the container arrived, but I sent my oldest daughter, Noel, to represent me. I'll never forget watching the news on CNN as Boris Yeltsin stood on top of a tank outside of the Russian White House during the early days of Russia's democracy. I prayed that my daughter would be safe.

When the World Help container arrived at the hospital, all of the doctors and nurses lined up in front of the building. Noel told me, "Dad, you wouldn't have believed it. While we were unloading the boxes, one of the surgeons ran out of the operating room, ripped open a box and grabbed a package of surgical tubing and said, 'I need this right now!' and then he immediately went back inside and saved someone's life.

"Dad," she said, "Dr. Mahkson put his hands on my shoulders and said, 'Young lady, please give your father a message from me. Please tell him that I said "thank you" for all of this help. And please, please tell him that you are the first Americans who have ever kept their promise to us.'"

Before we started helping Cancer Hospital #62, they had not received any outside help. These dedicated doctors and nurses were rinsing out latex gloves and using them over and over again—not the most sanitary of conditions. Can you imagine this happening here in the United States?

Since that day, we have sent 13 containers to Cancer Hospital #62 with medical supplies valued at nearly $2 million dollars.

Recently, one of our World Help Russian staff members was diagnosed with cancer. Because of the relationship we built with the cancer hospital, she was able to become a patient and receive the care she needed. One of the nurses even told her that the gurney she was lying on and many of the supplies used to treat her were donated through World

Help. She is a cancer survivor!

On one of my last visits to the hospital, Dr. Mahkson took me aside and said, "At first, I did not believe in your faith. But I have seen it in action and now I accept your faith."

God opened the door, World Help walked through it, and hundreds are not only being treated and cured of cancer but are accepting Jesus Christ because of this unconditional outpouring of love. They are *true* survivors—they will live forever!

I've been to Russia 42 times, building relationships every time I go. But I'll never forget the time I looked into the eyes of these patients suffering from cancer, shared my story, and helped make a difference in their lives.

Someone once asked me, "Did it ever occur to you that God is giving you a ministry to cancer patients?" I answered back, "Did it ever occur to you that I don't want a ministry to cancer patients?" "Why?" he asked. "Too painful!" But I have come to realize that God can turn your trial and

"Da Vinci painted one Mona Lisa. Beethoven composed one Fifth Symphony. And God made one version of you. He custom designed you for a one-of-a-kind assignment."

—Max Lucado[82]

tragedy into a platform to share His love and hope.

God's plan for the ministry of World Help didn't end with distributing Bibles and medical supplies in Russia.

Since our founding in 1991, we have touched lives in over 58 countries through our four pillars of ministry— Bible distribution, church planting, humanitarian aid and child sponsorship.

I realize that every new church we help plant, every container of food and clothing we share, every orphan we care for and every Bible we distribute is the direct result of my battle with cancer.

When I thought my life was over, I had no idea that God was actually giving me a brand new beginning and an incredible new ministry!

LIFE LESSONS LEARNED

The Triumph of My Tragedy

Place your life and future in God's hands. *"For I know the plans I have for you,' declares the LORD, 'plans to prosper you and not to harm you, plans to give you hope and a future'"* (Jeremiah 29:11).

Live one day at a time. Don't allow the uncertainties of life to consume you and shut you off from living and enjoying life. We are not promised tomorrow, so make the most of today.

Seek God's guidance and wisdom through prayer and Bible study. *"Trust in the Lord with all your heart; do not depend on your own understanding. Seek his will in all you do, and he will direct your paths"* (Proverbs 3:5-6, NLT).

God wants good things for you. God has already prepared treasures to replace your tragedy. If you are faithful, He will restore what you have lost and give you greater blessings than you could imagine—you will receive beauty for ashes. *"No good thing will the Lord withhold from those who do what is right"* (Psalm 84:11, NLT).

10

AFTER
THE STORM

Peace, Help and Hope for Tomorrow

"He will remove all their sorrows, and there will be no more death or sorrow or crying or pain, for the old world and its evils are gone forever."

—Revelation 21:4, NLT

I t was December 27, 2004, and I was as eager as any parent would be to hear my son pound away on the new drum set he had received for Christmas. Yeah, right!

I started my day with coffee and intently watched the news. Images flooded the screen of the horrific destruction left by the tsunami that hit along the southeastern coast of India and Asia the day before, and reports kept getting worse.

Almost immediately, everyone knew this was one of the worst natural disasters in human history.

I knew I couldn't wait any longer. Even though it was World Help's Christmas break and our employees were enjoying time off with their families, I called an emergency Leadership Team meeting. Our Christmas break, short as it was, was officially over. We worked feverishly to come up with a plan that would be the best use of our resources.

We quickly contacted our partners who lived and

worked in the tsunami zone to make sure everyone was all right and that all of the children we sponsor were safe. We strategized on how to get much-needed relief to them immediately.

As the days passed and reports were updated, the enormity of the destruction left after the tsunami overwhelmed us. The storm affected everyone—young and old, rich and poor. In a brief instant, a huge wall of water demolished entire villages, destroyed hundreds of thousands of homes, and left survivors devastated and homeless, wandering aimlessly in a state of indescribable grief. The tsunami claimed more than 220,000 lives; the actual death toll will probably never be known.

Our partners in the field sent us daily reports of what they witnessed firsthand and the overwhelming challenges they faced while providing relief to the survivors. They found a few families housed in dilapidated school buildings, huddled together under plastic sheets, trying to stay warm. There were heartbreaking stories of hundreds of families with no food, shelter, or safe water to drink. They were helpless.

The devastation was so widespread that help did not arrive in many of the hardest-hit locations for days, and for some ... weeks!

We were involved in providing tents for refugee camps, survival kits, food, medicine and teams of grief counselors. We identified 379 children in South Thailand who were affected by the disaster. The Thai government was more than willing to accept help, even from Christian organizations. We raised enough funds for a children's home—providing food, staff salaries, rent and vehicles for three years.

At that point, I decided it was time for me to personally visit the tsunami zone. I wanted to see the destruction for myself. I went with a small team, including my close friend and World Help Board member, Skip Taylor. We had provided food, shelter, and humanitarian aid, but now we wanted to do more—we wanted to help them rebuild.

Our goal on the trip to South India and Thailand was to have hands-on involvement in the distribution process, visit the villages where our partners were working, and let the survivors know that we cared for them and wanted to help them.

What I had seen on television, as heart-wrenching as it was, did not begin to prepare me for what I experienced. Everywhere we went, there were miles and miles of devastation. I have visited so many third world countries; I thought I would be prepared for the smells that the reporters talked about. But I wasn't. The sight and smell of decomposing human bodies and rotting animal carcasses was more overwhelming than I'd ever imagined.

Although I was excited to be on the ground, meeting people face-to-face, the shock of actually being there—smelling, seeing and touching—was heartbreaking. And it was just the beginning.

In the first village we visited, I stood on a heap of bricks and rubble to get a better view of the area. The frail man next to me quietly and slowly said, "I found my 7-year-old

"God is not an absentee Ruler who sits at His controls and pulls switches and punches buttons to make people and events dance like marionettes. Our God is a hands-on God."

—David Jeremiah[83]

boy under that pile of bricks. He was dead. I had to dig him out and bury him. It was one of the hardest things I ever had to do."

As we walked through another camp, I met one father who said he was holding his two children by the hand when the giant wave hit. He couldn't hold onto them as the surging waters ripped them from his arms. The last word he heard them speak was, "Father!" Their bodies were never recovered.

I couldn't even begin to imagine what these fathers must have felt! More than one-third of the tsunami victims were children. It was tragic.

Our teams of psychiatrists and grief counselors treated many people like 28-year-old Meenakshi, whose four children—ages 4 to 12—were swept away by a wall of water in the fishing village of Nagapattinam, India. While other survivors clamored for the rice we had brought, this guilt-ridden woman sat in the corner and stared vacantly toward the ocean.

"Why didn't God spare me even one?" she asked repeatedly.

There were countless stories of grief just like these, all of them so painful to hear.

We met for several hours with the leaders of the Bang Sak village in Phuket, Thailand, reviewing plans for rebuilding their homes. Their faces were a mix of excitement and disbelief that someone wanted to help them in such a tangible, long-term way—especially someone from halfway around the world. We were able to help them rebuild 20 houses. One of the biggest surprises for us was when we saw that the village chief had already set aside land for a church without us even asking. We earned the right to be heard, and God's hand was so evident!

The next day, we heard about a Muslim village north of Phuket that had been completely destroyed—entirely swept away. The survivors hadn't received any supplies since the initial drop four weeks earlier. They were totally forgotten! We quickly loaded a huge truck with food, gas stoves and many other supplies, and drove more than two hours to that forgotten village.

When we arrived, it seemed like everyone in the village came out to greet us with open arms. We found 78 devastated families with nothing but the clothes on their backs. The effects of not having food and supplies for weeks were evident—they were starving and their faces were sunken in. They looked so fragile. The chief thanked us over and over again—we became friends immediately.

We unloaded the truck and distributed the aid. We told

"(God gave you) a zone, a region, a life precinct in which you were made to dwell. He tailored the curves of your life to fit an empty space in his jigsaw puzzle. And life makes sweet sense when you find your spot."

—Max Lucado[84]

them we were Christians and that we wanted to help them in the name of Jesus. Their faces were full of gratefulness, relief and a hint of joy. They had been abandoned for weeks, but finally someone had brought them help.

I can't begin to explain what it felt like to be able to meet their most basic needs. I wasn't just unloading a truck, I was meeting a tremendous need—a need for survival. What would have happened to these men, women and children, had we not taken the time to go to them?

I believe that God had us there for that one forgotten village.

Later that day, I sat on the front porch of one of their makeshift houses and drank coffee with a Muslim cleric. We shared stories and talked about what life was like before the tsunami—and what the future might hold.

I realized that in the face of so much pain and devastation, God provided healing and hope. A Christian and a Muslim who otherwise would have never crossed paths were talking, laughing, crying and even praying together.

He had weathered his storm, and I had weathered mine. It was an incredible conversation. After much pain, God had given him help, peace and hope for tomorrow through World Help—the hope born out of my own tragedy.

We sat together in the quiet and peace after the storm.

⟡

As the cares of life are stripped away by challenges and turmoil, we can look deep inside our heart and soul and discover what really matters ... we can discover the passion God has planted within us. And as we step back and look at the path God has brought us along so far, we can see how His gentle hand has been guiding and preparing us all along for His divine purpose in our lives.

I pray that the lessons I've shared through my experience will help you find the answers you need to help you weather your storm—but more than that, to come out on the other side with great triumph!

Your story is unique, special and God-ordained. The struggles and heartbreaks of your life are important. You are more valuable than you could ever comprehend. What happens to you matters. God created you so painstakingly, so carefully, because He loves you. Can you believe He knows how many hairs are on your head?[85] God has a plan and a purpose for your life and the struggles you face are preparing you for the greatest triumph of your life.

After the Storm—
THE ANSWERS YOU NEED

Before we end our journey together, I want to make sure I have answered some of the questions you have as you face your storms of life. I want to help equip you with the confidence and courage you need for victory by sharing the answers I discovered.

Why? Why is this happening to me? As humans, we cannot know all the motivations that come into play during the tragedies of our lives. Much of the spirit world is beyond our knowledge or comprehension this side of eternity. Sometimes our trials are brought about by our own mistakes and failings ... sometimes they are meant to grow us spiritually, mentally or emotionally ... sometimes they are to let our faith shine for the benefit of ourselves and others. Even though the exact purpose may not be clear right now, you can know that as you go through a struggle God is preparing you for a greater purpose and plan for your life.

How? This is more than I can bear. I don't have the solutions. How am I going to get through this? Your situation may seem hopeless, but you have a greater strength within you than you are aware of. As a child of God, you have a reservoir of power and a future full of hope. Tap into your resources—prayer, God's Word, family and friends. Through the power and hope of Jesus Christ, you will get through this! You can gain strength from His unconditional love.

What? What's going to happen to me ... to my family ... to my life? No matter how many unknowns you face today, you can know beyond a shadow of a doubt that God is looking out for your future. He loves you. He loves your spouse. He loves your children. You can rest assured that God will lead and guide you every step of the way.

God cares so much for you that He has ordered the steps of your life and you can trust Him to complete the job. The storm you face will not overcome you. You are more than a conqueror.

Why?

How?

Through Christ Jesus. "We are more than conquerors through Him who loved us!"[86]

When I was facing death, I never realized what God had planned for my life. Today, as I travel around the world and meet people who are suffering unimaginable storms of life, I am thankful for my great trial—my battle with cancer. At the time, would I have chosen to endure the pain to get to this point in life?

I don't know.

But am I grateful for cancer? I can say, with all honesty, "Yes." It made me who I am today. I've experienced more joy, deeper friendships and greater purpose than I ever would have otherwise.

Not only is my work through World Help my divine purpose, it is also the passion of my heart. Catullus, the Roman poet, once said, "It is difficult to lay aside a confirmed passion."[07] Although methods and strategies have changed through the years, I have never been able to "lay aside" the passion that God gave me for reaching the world with the Gospel. IT IS THE TRIUMPH OF MY TRAGEDY!

11

GOD'S PROMISES

Throwing Out the Lifeline

God's Word has always been a source of encouragement and strength for me. But during the dark days of my struggle with cancer, its promises and lessons took on an even greater meaning in my life. I clung to the hope and peace I found in Scripture. Sometimes as I opened His Word, I literally felt the presence of God sheltering me from the storm.

ANGER

"Be quick to listen, slow to speak and slow
to become angry."
JAMES 1:19

"Anger resides in the lap of fools."
ECCLESIASTES 7:9

"Don't let evil get the best of you, but conquer
evil by doing good."
ROMANS 12:21, NLT

ANXIETY

"God is our refuge and strength, an ever-present
help in trouble."
PSALM 46:1

"The Lord your God is with you, he is mighty to save ...
he will quiet you with his love."
ZEPHANIAH 3:17

"Don't worry about anything; instead pray
about everything."
PHILIPPIANS 4:6-7, NLT

BITTERNESS

"Refrain from anger and turn from wrath; do not fret—
it leads only to evil."
PSALM 37:8

"He who refreshes others will himself be refreshed."
PROVERBS 11:25

"Get rid of all bitterness, rage, anger, harsh words, and
slander, as well as all types of malicious behavior."
EPHESIANS 4:31, NLT

COMFORT

"I will not leave you comfortless: I will come to you."
JOHN 14:18, KJV

"The LORD is my rock, my fortress and my
deliverer; my God is my rock, in whom I take refuge."
PSALM 18:2

"Though he stumble, he will not fall, for the LORD
upholds him with his hand."
PSALM 37:24

"Cast your cares on the LORD and he will sustain you;
he will never let the righteous fall."
PSALM 55:22

CONTENTMENT

"Keep your lives free from the love of money and
be content with what you have."
HEBREWS 13:5

"Godliness with contentment is great gain."
I TIMOTHY 6:6

"I am not saying this because I am in need,
for I have learned to be content whatever
the circumstances."
PHILIPPIANS 4:11

DEATH

"Even when I walk through the dark valley of death,
I will not be afraid,
for you are close beside me. Your rod and your staff
protect and comfort me."

PSALM 23:4, NLT

"Blessed are those who mourn, for they
will be comforted."

MATTHEW 5:4

"That is why we never give up. Though our bodies
are dying, our spirits are being renewed every day."

II CORINTHIANS 4:16, NLT

DEPRESSION

"The LORD is a shelter for the oppressed, a refuge
in times of trouble."

PSALM 9:9, NLT

"A cheerful look brings joy to the heart, and good
news gives health to the bones."

PROVERBS 15:30

"You will fill me with joy in your presence."
PSALM 16:11

DISCOURAGEMENT

"Come to me, all you who are weary and burdened,
and I will give you rest."
MATTHEW 11:28

"You hear, O Lord, the desire of the afflicted; you
encourage them, and you listen to their cry."
PSALM 10:17

"The Lord upholds all those who fall and lifts up
all who are bowed down."
PSALM 145:14

FAITH

"Faith is being sure of what we hope for and certain
of what we do not see."
HEBREWS 11:1

"The Lord preserves the faithful."
PSALM 31:23

"Now for a little while you may have had to suffer grief in all kinds of trials. These have come so that your faith ... may be proved genuine."
1 PETER 1:6-7

"So then faith comes by hearing and hearing by the Word of God."
ROMANS 10:17, NKJV

FEAR

"Do not fear ... I will help you."
ISAIAH 41:13

"And we know that God causes everything to work together for the good of those who love God and are called according to his purpose for them."
ROMANS 8:28, NLT

"When you lie down, you will not be afraid; when you lie down, your sleep will be sweet."
PROVERBS 3:24

"Even though I walk through the valley of the shadow of death, I will fear no evil, for you are with me; your rod and your staff, they comfort me."
PSALM 23:4

FORGIVENESS

"Everyone who believes in Jesus receives forgiveness
of sins through his name."
ACTS 10:43

"If we confess our sins, God is faithful and just and
will forgive us our sins."
1 JOHN 1:9

"You are forgiving and good, O Lord, abounding in
love to all who call to you."
PSALM 86:5

HOPE

"The faith and love that spring from the hope that
is stored up for you in heaven."
COLOSSIANS 1:5

"Be strong and take heart, all you who hope in the LORD."
PSALM 31:24

"We wait in hope for the LORD; he is our help
and our shield."
Psalm 33:20

INSECURITY

"For you, Lord, have never forsaken those who seek you."
PSALM 9:10

"The Lord is good. When trouble comes,
he is a strong refuge."
NAHUM 1:7, NLT

"Trust in the Lord forever ... the Lord,
is the Rock eternal."
ISAIAH 26:4

LONELINESS

"And be sure of this: I am with you always,
even to the end of the age."
MATTHEW 28:20, NLT

"The Lord is close to all who call on him, yes,
to all who call on him sincerely."
PSALM 145:18, NLT

"Then you will call, and the Lord will answer; you will
cry for help, and he will say: Here am I."
ISAIAH 58:9

"I am with you and will watch over you wherever
you go ... I will not leave you."
GENESIS 28:15

LOVE

"God has poured out his love into our hearts."
ROMANS 5:5

"Because of the Lord's great love, we are not consumed."
LAMENTATIONS 3:22-23

"Jesus said, 'Love one another. As I have loved you.'"
JOHN 13:34

PATIENCE

"Be strong and take heart and wait for the LORD."
PSALM 27:14

"Hold unswervingly to the hope we profess,
for God ... is faithful."
HEBREWS 10:23

"Love is patient."
1 CORINTHIANS 13:4

PEACE

"My unfailing love for you will not be shaken nor my
covenant of peace be removed."
ISAIAH 54:10

"His peace will guard your hearts and minds
as you live in Christ Jesus."
PHILIPPIANS 4:7, NLT

"I am leaving you with a gift—peace of mind and heart.
And the peace I give isn't like the peace the world gives.
So don't be troubled or afraid."
JOHN 14:27, NLT

"A heart at peace gives life to the body."
PROVERBS 14:30

PRAYER

"For everyone who asks, receives. Everyone who seeks,
finds. And the door is opened to everyone who knocks."
MATTHEW 7:7-8, NLT

"If you believe, you will receive whatever you ask
for in prayer."
MATTHEW 21:22

"The earnest prayer of a righteous person has great
power and wonderful results."
JAMES 5:16, NLT

"The LORD ... hears the prayers of the righteous."
PROVERBS 15:29, NLT

PROTECTION

"You are my hiding place, Lord; you will protect
me from trouble."
PSALM 32:7

"He guards the course of the just and protects
the way of his faithful ones."
PROVERBS 2:6-8

"I am with you and will watch over you
wherever you go."
GENESIS 28:15

UNCERTAINTY

"Everyone born of God overcomes the world."
1 JOHN 5:4

"For God did not give us a spirit of timidity, but a spirit
of power, of love and of self-discipline."
II TIMOTHY 1:7

"The LORD hears his people when they call to him for
help. He rescues them from all their troubles."
PSALM 34:17, NLT

WAITING

"The Lord is wonderfully good to those who wait
for him and seek him."
LAMENTATIONS 3:25-26, NLT

"Wait patiently for the Lord.
Be brave and courageous."
PSALM 27:14, NLT

"Wait for the Lord and he will save you."
PROVERBS 20:22, NKJV

WISDOM

"If any of you lacks wisdom, he should ask God …
and it will be given to him."
JAMES 1:5

"I will instruct you and teach you in the
way you should go."
PSALM 32:8

"To the man who pleases him, God gives wisdom,
knowledge and happiness."
ECCLESIASTES 2:26

ENDNOTES

1   The White House, "Proclamation by the President: National Day of Prayer and Remembrance for the Victims of Hurricane Katrina," news release, September 8, 2005, http://www.whitehouse.gov/news/releases/2005/09/print/20050908-12.html.

2   C.S. Lewis, http://www.quotedb.com/quotes/594.

3   *Cancer Facts & Figures 2006*, American Cancer Society, Atlanta, 2006 http://www.cancer.org/downloads/STT/CAFF2006PWSecured.pdf.

4   James 1:2.

5   John Eldredge, *Wild at Heart,* page 176, Thomas Nelson, Inc. 2001.

6   Job 1:13-19.

7   Job 1:8.

8   Job 1:22.

9   Galatians 6:7, James 1:13-16.

10   Romans 6:15-16.

11   John 15:20, I Peter 4:12.

12   James 1:1-3.

13   "Church Information/Resources," Persecution.org, http://www.persecution.org/newsite/churchresources.php.

14   Ron Strom, "Faith Under Fire: Group tireless in supporting persecuted church," WorldNetDaily, June 23, 2005, http://wnd.com/news/article.asp?ARTICLE_ID=44911.

15   Jeff King, "Three Christian High School Girls Beheaded— Persecution in Indonesia Takes Dramatic Turn for the Worse," Persecution.org, November 3, 2005, http://www.persecution.org/newsite/pressdetail.php?presscode=107.

16   Composers: Scott Wesley Brown & Greg Nelson c. 1985 Laurel Press and New Wings Music, Pamela Kay Music, Greg Nelson Music. http://members.aol.com/Mbr8778/strengthofthelord.html

17   C.S. Lewis, *A Grief Observed*, 1961 Faber and Faber, London, under the pseudonym N. W. Clerk.

18   Charles Spurgeon http://www.weeks-g.dircon.co.uk/quotes_by_author_s.htm.

19   Jeremiah 29:11, Romans 8:28.

20   Romans 8:28.

21   Isaiah 43:2.

22   Lee Cowan, "Five Years Later, 9/11's Survivors: Victims Struggle To Move On," CBS Sunday Morning, CBS News. September 11, 2006. http://www.cbsnews.com/stories/2006/09/10/sunday/main1990770.shtml.

23   Isaiah 43:19.

24   Charles Swindoll, http://www.worldofquotes.com/topic/Cliches-and-One~Liners/index.html.

25   Psalm 46:1, Philippians 4:13, Romans 8:37.

26   H. P. Lovecraft, 1927 essay "Supernatural Horror in Literature," http://en.wikiquote.org/wiki/Fear.

27   Hebrews 9:27.

28   John Quincy Adams, 6th President, http://thinkexist.com/search/
     searchquotation.asp?search=patience&page=1.

29   James 1:3.

30   I Peter 1:7.

31   James 1:3.

32   Afterhours Inspirational Stories. "Don't Give Up" Author
     Unknown, Source Unknown. http://www.inspirationalstories.com/
     6/610.html.

33   Winston Churchill, British Prime Minister during WWII,
     http://thinkexist.com/quotations/motivation/.

34   Corrie Ten Boom, "Dealing with Doubt," RPM Ministries "Quotes
     of Note" http://www.rpmbooks.org/quotes.html#dealing.

35   Isaiah 50:7.

36   David Jeremiah, *Prayer, the Great Adventure*, page 19,
     Multnomah Publishers, Inc., 1997.

37   Dave Earley, *Prayer Odyssey*, pages 167-169, Destiny Image
     Publishers, Inc., 2003.

38   Jeremiah, page 41.

39   Matthew 18:19.

40   Catherine Rauch, "Probing the power of prayer" January 18, 2000,
     CNN.com http://archives.cnn.com/2000/HEALTH/
     alternative/01/18/prayer.power.wmd/.

41   Matthew 6:7-8.

42   Max Lucado, "Hurry Up and Pray: The Importance of Waiting for

God's Power," *Today's Christian*, November/December 2004 issue, http://www.christianitytoday.com/tc/2005/001/4.35.html.

43   J. Otis Ledbetter, *In the Secret Place*, page 12, Multnomah Publishers, Inc., 2003.

44   John 11:41-42.

45   Philippians 4:6-7.

46   2 Thessalonians 3:1-2.

47   Matthew 7:7-8.

48   Matthew 7:9-11.

49   Matthew 26:39.

50   Billy Graham, http://www.worldofquotes.com/topic/Cliches-and-One~Liners/index.html.

51   Isaiah 41:10.

52   Romans 8:31, 1 John 4:4, Isaiah 55:10-11.

53   Matthew 16:18, NKJV.

54   Philippians 4:6-7.

55   2 Timothy 4:7-8.

56   C.S. Lewis, http://www.brainyquote.com/quotes/authors/c/c_s_lewis.html.

57   "No Reserves. No Retreats. No Regrets," http://home.snu.edu/~HCULBERT/regret.htm, reprinted from *Daily Bread*, December 31, 1988, and The Yale Standard, Fall 1970 edition.

58   Max Lucado, http://www.worldofquotes.com/topic/

Cliches-and-One~Liners/index.html.

59   Ephesians 4:11-13.

60   James 1:4.

61   A.W. Tozer, "Suffering, Sorrow, Pain, Perseverance,
     God's Purposes and Spirituality," RPM Ministries,
     "Quotes of Note," http://www.rpmbooks.org/quotes.html.

62   Charles H. Spurgeon, quoted in "Streams in the Desert,"
     quoted in "Reflections," *Christianity Today*, June 16, 1997, p. 45,
     http://www.bible.org/illus.asp?topic_id=1509.

63   Corrie Ten Boom, Wikipedia.
     http://en.wikipedia.org/wiki/Corrie_ten_Boom.

64   Lady Bird Johnson, http://www.worldofquotes.com/topic/
     Cliches-and-One~Liners/index.html.

65   In Touch Ministries http://www.intouch.org/
     myintouch/mighty/portraits/corrie_ten_boom_159770.html.

66   Ibid.

67   James 1:12.

68   http://www.flemingmultimedia.com/Personal/CSA/monument.html

69   C.S. Lewis,
     http://www.brainyquote.com/quotes/authors/c/c_s_lewis.html.

70   Martin Luther King Jr., http://www.brainyquote.com/
     quotes/quotes/m/martinluth105087.html

71   Andrae Crouch, "Through It All,"
     http://www.selahonline.com/lyrics_hidingplace.html.
     © 1971 Renewed 1999 Manna Music, Inc. 35255 Brooten Road,
     Pacific City, OR 97135.

72 Dr. Paul Brand, *Fearfully and Wonderfully Made*, Zondervan, 1987.

73 Matthew 9:36, NKJV.

74 Robert Pierce, "Missions, Slogans and Quotes from Missionaries," http://home.snu.edu/~hculbert/slogans.htm.

75 Matthew 14:13-21.

76 Matthew 9:36-38.

77 Luke 19:10.

78 John 21:15-17, NKJV.

79 Billy Graham, http://thinkexist.com/quotation/god_has_given_us_two_hands-one_to_receive_with/296925.html.

80 John Piper, http://en.thinkexist.com/quotes/john_piper/.

81 C.S. Lewis, http://www.brainyquote.com/quotes/authors/c/c_s_lewis.html.

82 Max Lucado, *Cure for the Common Life*, excerpt from Chapter 1, page 2, Wesleyan Publishing House, 2006, http://www.maxlucado.com/cure/.

83 Jeremiah, page 176.

84 Lucado, page 2.

85 Luke 12:7.

86 Romans 8:37.

87 http://creativequotations.com/one/1690.htm.

ABOUT THE AUTHOR

*"Every day, I try to live my life in such a way that I
accomplish at least one thing that will outlive me and
last for eternity."*

—Vernon Brewer,
Personal Mission Statement

VERNON BREWER is the founder and president of World Help, a non-profit, nondenominational Christian organization that was founded to meet the spiritual and physical needs of hurting people around the world.

Vernon is also author of *The Forgotten Children: Hungry. Hopeless. Running for their lives.* This eye-opening book shares the heartbreaking story of the war-ravaged children of Northern Uganda.

"I wish that all Christians could see the world as I have seen it ... to actually see firsthand the masses of hurting people, the hungry and orphaned children, the displaced families, the lepers, the poor, as well as experience the smells and sounds. But even more than that, I wish for you to see the world through the eyes of God."

His incredible life experiences, combined with his passion for the unreached peoples of the world, make him an energetic and compassionate leader. His strategic thinking and emphasis on partnership have breathed new life into the mission world and provided innovative ways to partner together and accomplish more for the Kingdom of God.

Vernon has conducted international evangelistic campaigns and rallies in over 50 foreign countries worldwide, as well as numerous leadership training conferences in Uganda, China, India, Nepal, Burma, Romania and Russia. In addition, he has personally taken over 4,000 people to the mission field. He has led over 500 local church evangelistic rallies, and has lectured on 30 college and university campuses. He has spoken to over 1 million teenagers in public high school assembly programs, and is a frequent speaker at camps and conferences.

Vernon's personal testimony of his struggle with cancer has been a source of encouragement to many people facing difficult situations.

ABOUT WORLD HELP

World Help is a nonprofit, nondenominational Christian organization that exists to fulfill the Great Commission and the Great Commandment through partnering, training, helping and serving, especially in the unreached areas of the world.

We do this through four pillars of ministry—Bible distribution, church planting, humanitarian aid and child sponsorship.

Since our founding in 1991, World Help has touched over 58 countries through our ministries. We have seen and responded to the spiritual and humanitarian needs of people groups around the world. This is how we offer help and hope:

HUMANITARIAN AID. God loves and cares about suffering people. And if we share God's heart, we must see the world through His eyes ... a world in need.

Hunger, war, famine, disease and natural disaster create a worldwide climate of suffering that most of us cannot begin to comprehend.

World Help has seen firsthand the incredible suffering and hardships that people around the world endure every day of their lives. It is our desire to meet the physical needs of hurting people around the world and in so doing ... earn the right to be heard!

With the support of individuals, churches, organizations and medical facilities, World Help has shipped over 108 ocean-going containers and distributed critically needed humanitarian aid worldwide at an estimated value of $61 million.

ESTABLISH CHURCHES. *"Go and make disciples of all nations"* was the last command Jesus gave His disciples. Jesus did not command us to do the impossible, nor did He command us to go to the ends of the earth with His Gospel if He did not expect us to obey. However, today there are still entire groups of people who have never heard of Jesus Christ.

Church-planting movements are the key to evangelizing the least-reached peoples of the world. Utilizing national church planters, effective church-planting movements penetrate entire people groups with the Gospel. It is the vision of World Help to help plant indigenous, reproducing churches where no churches currently exist. To date, God has allowed our partners to plant over 31,000 churches in the unreached areas of the world.

LOVE CHILDREN. Millions of people around the world suffer hardship, hunger and disease. But those who suffer the most are the children. They endure unimaginable living conditions on a daily basis without any hope of a better future.

In the face of these great needs one can feel overwhelmed. World Help's Child Sponsorship Program was born out of the desire to "change the world ... one child at a time." World Help has provided over 19,000 sponsorships for children in desperate need around the world. A sponsor can provide a child with the basic necessities ... food, clothing, medical attention and educational opportunities. Most importantly, these children receive the message that God loves them and has a special plan for their lives.

PROVIDE BIBLES. World Help has witnessed an immense hunger for God's Word all around the world. Thousands risk their lives every day for the sake of the Gospel. Pastors, church leaders, Christians of all nationalities plead with us to provide them with Bibles ... and we can help them!

The Bible is the most powerful tool God has given us to reach the souls of lost people throughout our world. It is the most important resource we can place in any believer's hand.

World Help was founded on fulfilling this most basic and desperate need. Since inception, we have printed and distributed more than 8 million Bibles, New Testaments and other pieces of Christian literature to places where they are needed the most.

"Thousands have partnered with World Help and God has allowed us to see countless lives miraculously changed ... thousands of churches planted in places where there were none ... children receiving help and

hope through sponsorships ... and millions of Bibles provided to those who have never seen a Bible, much less owned one. Together, we are committed to sharing Christ's love, His hope and peace with the unreached people of this world."

—*Vernon Brewer*

World Help is also committed to faithful stewardship of funds entrusted to us by donors. We promise to use your gifts wisely and effectively in Christ's name and provide information, a network of international contacts, and financial and ministry accountability for each mission project in which we participate. World Help strives to keep overhead costs to a minimum using only 9% for the administration of our various projects. All gifts designated for specific projects are used as designated. To ensure our financial accountability to you, World Help is a member of the Evangelical Council for Financial Accountability (ECFA) and an annual financial report is readily available for anyone requesting a copy.

For more information about World Help and our outreaches and programs and to learn how you can join us in carrying out the Great Commission and the Great Commandment, visit our website at **www.worldhelp.net**.

WHAT OTHERS ARE SAYING ABOUT VERNON BREWER AND WORLD HELP

"World Help is making a positive spiritual impact in Eastern Europe and deserves your support."

THE LATE BILL BRIGHT,
founder, Campus Crusade for Christ International

"I applaud heartily what Vernon Brewer and World Help are doing: mobilizing churches in the USA towards church planting via good/focused relationships with local ministry partners overseas. This does not come readily or easy! This comes from broad, experienced involvement and credentials gained with time, which Vernon and World Help have exemplified. Praise God! Many blessings as it continues!"

LUIS BUSH,
founder, AD 2000 and Beyond Movement
and Global Inquiry

"World Help is a strategic organization for world evangelism. I appreciate the leadership of Vernon Brewer and the experience and passion that he brings to missions."

DR. ED DOBSON,
retired pastor, Calvary Church, Grand Rapids, Michigan

"It's been my distinct privilege to travel and co-labor with Vernon. What a delight to hear and see Vernon's passion for a global gospel presentation. Vernon and World Help are doing things many dream about. I pray God greatly blesses Vernon and the ongoing ministry of World Help."

MICHAEL EASLEY,
president, Moody Bible Institute

I have partnered with Vernon Brewer and World Help in Russia and Cuba. I believe in this ministry and their passion and vision to reach this world for Christ.

JOSH MCDOWELL,
author and communicator

"Vernon Brewer was the first graduate of Liberty University and served here for many years as Vice President of Student Affairs. For the past 15 years he has served as the president of World Help, an international relief and missions ministry headquartered here in the Lynchburg area. Vernon is one of the leading missionary statesmen of our times. In almost every major international crisis, he is the first to respond with both the Gospel and significant relief efforts. We are proud of Vernon. He is one of our finest alumni."

DR. JERRY FALWELL,
founder and chancellor, Liberty University

"I have known Vernon Brewer for quite some time. His work in missions and preparing young people has been effective and important. He knows about the fields available today ... and I am pleased to recommend his ministry."

LARRY JONES,
co-founder, Feed the Children

I enthusiastically recommend World Help, and I have great confidence in Vernon Brewer. I have known him for over 20 years, and I have worked with him shoulder-to-shoulder in the work of the kingdom. No one has stirred my heart for the work of missions as much as this outstanding man of God.

JAY STRACK,
former vice-president, Southern Baptist Convention

"Vernon, thank you for responding to the call of God. You responded ... you did something when He called you, and He gave you an extended life. You didn't just go back to the same old, same old ... you did something that is going to make a huge impact and you're doing it and we thank you. God loves you and so do we!"

REV. DR. ROBERT A. SCHULLER,
pastor, Crystal Cathedral, Garden Grove, California

"World Help is a proven servant to the churches of Eastern Europe."

LUIS PALAU,
international evangelist

"World Help is providing a means for Christians to touch the world ... they are doing what Jesus commanded us to do. God bless them!"

ROGER BRELAND,
founder, TRUTH

STAY INFORMED!

Keep updated on all that you are accomplishing around the world through the many outreaches of World Help ...

... by logging onto www.worldhelp.net!

Our high-impact website will inform and inspire you! Take a look for yourself and you will be amazed at the colorful presentations ... the heart-touching stories and testimonies ... the incredible photography ... and the exciting on-line videos. This user-friendly site will take you through the many ministries and outreaches of World Help, as we share our vision and background, and let you know of opportunities that will allow you to step into the mission field from your own home. Check us out!

... by signing up for regular email reports!

Sign up today to receive regular updates and information about the outreaches and ministry opportunities of World Help via email. It's so quick and easy ... just go online at www.worldhelp.net and click on the "World Help Emails" icon. You will receive regular reports on the impact we are making around the world together in Christ's name.

Get your FREE
HOPE MAGAZINE
subscription!

This quarterly magazine will keep you updated on all our global work together. You will see vivid, 4-color photos of the very people you are impacting and read incredible testimonies of how God is using World Help through the prayers and support of friends like you.

This quality news publication will also address the latest issues, reports and needs from around the world and show how World Help is involved.

To view the latest issues of HOPE Magazine or sign up for your FREE subscription, go to www.worldhelp.net and click on "HOPE Magazine" under the "Get Involved" listing.